D1243500

Politics and Power in the UK

Power, Dissent, Equality: Understanding Contemporary Politics

This book is part of a series produced by Edinburgh University Press in association with The Open University. The complete list of books in the series is as follows:

What is Politics?
Jef Huysmans

Exploring Political Worlds
Edited by Paul Lewis

Politics and Power in the UK
Edited by Richard Heffernan and Grahame Thompson

Living Political Ideas
Edited by Geoff Andrews and Michael Saward

Making Policy, Shaping Lives
Edited by Raia Prokhovnik

The books form part of an Open University course DD203 *Power, Dissent, Equality: Understanding Contemporary Politics*. Details of this and other Open University courses can be obtained from the Course Information and Advice Centre, PO Box 724, The Open University, Milton Keynes MK7 6ZS, United Kingdom: tel. +44 (0)1908 653231, e-mail general-enquiries@open.ac.uk

Alternatively, you may visit the Open University website at www.open.ac.uk where you can learn more about the wide range of courses and packs offered at all levels by The Open University.

For availability of other course components visit the webshop at www.ouw.co.uk, or contact Open University Worldwide, Michael Young Building, Walton Hall, Milton Keynes MK7 6AA, United Kingdom for a brochure. tel. +44 (0)1908 858785; fax +44 (0)1908 858787; e-mail ouwenq@open.ac.uk

Politics and Power
in the UK

Edited by
Richard Heffernan and Grahame Thompson

Edinburgh University Press

in association with

The Open
University

Edinburgh University Press Ltd
22 George Square, Edinburgh

First published 2005 by Edinburgh University Press Ltd; written and produced by
The Open University

© 2005 The Open University

Edited, designed and typeset by The Open University.

Printed and bound in the United Kingdom by the Alden Group, Oxford.

All rights reserved. No part of this publication may be reproduced, stored in a retrieval
system, transmitted or utilized in any form or by any means, electronic, mechanical,
photocopying, recording or otherwise, without written permission from the publisher
or a licence from the Copyright Licensing Agency Ltd. Details of such licences (for
reprographic reproduction) may be obtained from the Copyright Licensing Agency Ltd
of 90 Tottenham Court Road, London W1T 4LP.

Open University course materials may also be made available in electronic formats for
use by students of the University. All rights, including copyright and related rights and
database rights, in electronic course materials and their contents are owned by or
licensed to The Open University, or otherwise used by The Open University as
permitted by applicable law.

In using electronic course materials and their contents you agree that your use will be
solely for the purposes of following an Open University course of study or otherwise
as licensed by The Open University or its assigns.

Except as permitted above you undertake not to copy, store in any medium (including
electronic storage or use in a website), distribute, transmit or re-transmit, broadcast,
modify or show in public such electronic materials in whole or in part without the
prior written consent of The Open University or in accordance with the Copyright,
Designs and Patents Act 1988.

A CIP record for this book is available from the British Library.

ISBN 0 7486 1969 0 (hardback)

ISBN 0 7486 1970 4 (paperback)

1.1

Contents

Preface   vii

INTRODUCTION   1

Powers & structures

CHAPTER 1
Governing at the centre: the politics of the parliamentary state   5
Richard Heffernan

Centre & periphery

CHAPTER 2
Centre–periphery relations: government beyond Westminster   41
Montserrat Guibernau

Participation & dissent

CHAPTER 3
Citizens and politics: modes of participation and dissent   75
Mads Qvortrup

Equality & difference

CHAPTER 4
Policy networks and interest representation   105
Grahame Thompson

Evidence & argument

CHAPTER 5
Analysing politics: constitutional reform   137
Jeremy Mitchell

Acknowledgements   167

Index   169

The Open University course team

Geoff Andrews, *Staff Tutor in Government and Politics*

Brian Ashcroft, *Associate Lecturer Panel*

Pam Berry, *Compositor*

Karen Bridge, *Media Project Manager*

Vivienne Brown, *Professor of Intellectual History*

Julie Charlesworth, *Lecturer, Open University Business School*

Martin Chiverton, *Media Production Specialist*

Stephen Clift, *Editor*

Lene Connolly, *Print Buyer*

John Craig, *Associate Lecturer Panel*

Michael Dawson, *Course Manager*

Marilyn Denman, *Secretary*

Andrew Dobson, *Professor of Politics*

Lucy Flook, *Course Manager*

Fran Ford, *Course Secretary*

Liz Freeman, *Copublishing Advisor*

Robert Garson, *Reader in American Studies*

Pam Garthwaite, *Course Manager*

Carl Gibbard, *Graphic Designer*

Bram Gieben, *Staff Tutor in Government and Politics*

Janis Gilbert, *Graphic Artist*

Richard Golden, *Production and Presentation Administrator*

Montserrat Guibernau, *Reader in Politics*

Lisa Hale, *Compositor*

Celia Hart, *Picture Researcher*

Richard Heffernan, *Lecturer in Government and Politics*

Wendy Humphreys, *Staff Tutor in Government and Politics*

Jef Huysmans, *Lecturer in Government and Politics*

Bob Kelly, *Staff Tutor in Government and Politics*

Paul Lewis, *Reader in Central and European Politics*

Joanna Mack, *Media Production Specialist*

David Middleton, *Staff Tutor in Government and Politics*

Jeremy Mitchell, *Lecturer in Government and Politics*

Raia Prokhovnik, *Senior Lecturer in Government and Politics and Deputy Course Team Chair*

Michael Saward, *Professor in Politics and Course Team Chair*

David Shulman, *BBC Producer*

Lynne Slocombe, *Editor*

Mark J. Smith, *Senior Lecturer in Government and Politics*

Grahame Thompson, *Professor of Political Economy*

Consultant authors

Richard Freeman, *Senior Lecturer in Politics, University of Edinburgh*

Deborah Mabbett, *Lecturer in Politics, Brunel University*

Mads Qvortrup, *Professor of Sociology and Public Policy, The Robert Gordon University, Aberdeen*

Judith Squires, *Senior Lecturer in Politics, University of Bristol*

Nicholas Watson, *Professor of Disability Studies, University of Glasgow*

External assessor

Michael Moran, *Professor of Government, University of Manchester*

Preface

Tumultuous events such as '9-11' and the war and its aftermath in Iraq have reminded people how critical – and sometimes how deadly – the world of politics can be. Even the local, everyday politics of council services, schools and hospitals can affect people's lives powerfully. The Open University, with its unique tradition of interdisciplinary work and its mission to reach and enthuse a hugely diverse student audience, has set out to show why and how politics matters. It aims to shed light on the inner workings of power, decision making and protest, covering politics from parliament to the street, from ideas to institutions. *Politics and Power in the UK* questions how we might make sense of major developments and debates in UK politics, such as devolution, constitutional change, changing patterns of citizen participation and the role of networks. It provides highly accessible insights into continuity and change in the ways in which power and participation work in the UK, and reflects with critical clarity on the methods and assumptions we use to study UK politics and government.

Series preface

This book is one of the five texts which make up the new *Power, Dissent, Equality: Understanding Contemporary Politics* series from The Open University. Each book in the series is designed for students and others who have not studied politics before, and can stand alone as a short introduction to key areas of debate within political science. However, if you wish to use the series as a whole, there are a number of references to chapters in other books in the series and these are easily identifiable because they are printed in bold type.

Each book offers a distinctive angle on the character and analysis of politics today. *What is Politics?* offers a critical overview, showing the often surprising faces and locations of political life. *Exploring Political Worlds* examines comparative politics, asking what we can learn by looking at one country or context in the light of another. *Politics and Power in the UK* questions how we might make sense of major developments and debates in UK politics, such as devolution and constitutional change. *Living Political Ideas* is an accessible introduction to key topics in political theory and ideology, such as legitimacy, national self-determination, dissent and social justice. *Making Policy, Shaping Lives* teases out and interrogates the many faces of public policy and policy making, drawing on case materials ranging from the single European currency to disability politics.

For all of the books, apart from *What is Politics?*, the chapters follow a common thematic structure. There are five organizing themes. *Powers and structures* explores the meaning and location of power in contemporary societies – what it is, and who has it. *Centre and periphery* looks at issues from the role of the state in our lives to the revival of nationalism in the post-Cold War world. *Participation and dissent* leads us to look, on the one hand, at voting and elections, and on the other hand at new and unconventional forms of political protest and dissent. *Equality and difference* examines how we are seen as 'equal to' and 'different from' each other and how this matters politically. The *evidence and argument* theme focuses attention on the ways in which the study of politics involves both explanation and recommendation.

Courses produced by The Open University are very much a team effort, and *Power, Dissent, Equality: Understanding Contemporary Politics* is no exception. Each member of the course team has made his or her mark on these books, and the work was done with goodwill and good humour. Some special thanks are owed. Raia Prokhovnik's tireless and dedicated contribution as Deputy and Acting Course Chair has been of huge benefit to the course. Mike Dawson has been a superbly calm, tactful and efficient Course Manager. Lucy Flook, Course Manager in the early days, played a significant role in getting the team up and running efficiently and ahead of schedule. Pam Garthwaite kept the momentum going in the period between Lucy's departure and Mike's arrival. The editorial skills of Stephen Clift and Lynne Slocombe and designs by Carl Gibbard have been key to the quality of the texts. Fran Ford has been a great support as course secretary, ably supported at different times by June Ayres and Marilyn Denman. John Craig and Brian Ashcroft have constituted a 'tutor panel' which has commented most helpfully on draft chapters. Robert Garson (Bobby) of Keele University was an influential and insightful member of the course team for two years. Professor Mick Moran of the University of Manchester has been the ideal external examiner – sharp and committed, he has been a tremendously positive influence on the content of these books.

Michael Saward, Course Team Chair

Introduction

Richard Heffernan and Grahame Thompson

This book investigates key issues of continuity and change in UK politics: how power is structured, how change is managed and disputed, and how observers have analysed the subject. In exploring these issues we consider core aspects of how the state works and how it is linked to society at large. The chapters examine the role of actors and institutions within central government, the relationships between central and peripheral government actors, the electoral relationship between the state and its citizens, how networks of numerous public, semi-public and private actors impact on the practice of politics and, finally, approaches to constitutional reform in the UK. This choice of topics is driven in part by the five themes we explore – powers and structures, centre and periphery, participation and dissent, equality and difference, and evidence and argument. The book cannot offer a comprehensive treatment of these topics; the chapters cover selected key issues, focusing on current debates about their significance and consequences.

The UK is a nation-state with a recognized territory and an established – if evolving – governance structure. It is recognized as a democracy, characterized by a state-enforced rule of law. Those actors and institutions which frame these laws have to be held accountable in some way to the community in whose name they govern. The state should be distinguished from the government: the state comprises the permanent features of UK governance; and the government comprises the set of elected officials operating at its core, given the right to manage and determine the state's day-to-day activities with the consent of parliament.

There are many definitions of politics but one that is useful in terms of investigating the state's actions and operations is to see it as a process of determining 'who gets what, when, how, and why'. Politics also often involves study of 'who does what to whom, when, and why?' This not only leads us to examine the activities of the state and its professional, practising politicians and bureaucrats, but also encourages us to consider the government roles played by citizens and interests operating beyond the state. States and governments are not separate from or autonomous of society: they impact on it, and are impacted on by it. Unlike authoritarian and totalitarian states, liberal democratic states such as the UK are connected to – indeed, are permeated by – citizens and opinion makers and by numerous non-state organizations which seek, with varying degrees of success, to influence and determine government policy. Among such organizations we may count political parties, pressure and interest groups, media organizations and national and international corporations. The study of politics prompts an understanding of the activities of the state (the institutions that administer and help regulate public affairs) and civil society (the individuals and interests who separately and collectively produce social life).

In liberal democracies the principal *formal* linkage between the state and society is free and fair elections. Other *informal* linkages also come into play, however, including the needs and demands of the market economy and the corporations operating within and around it, the dominant set of political and economic ideas that prescribe what policies the state should pursue and why, and the pressures of events and opinions that require states to mobilize in defence of what they see as their national interests. Against the background of these linkages political opinion is *directly* and *indirectly* represented within the state by a number of actors and activities, foremost among them the political parties and electoral processes, pressure groups and corporate interests. In addition, the news media, being both free to interpret critically the activities of government and to transmit information and opinion to citizens about what it does, acts as a check on the power of the state vis-à-vis civil society.

Varied interests lobby the state, either to try to influence it to do something, or to stop it from doing something. All state and non-state actors have some political resources, including wealth, income, status, position, prestige, organization, information and education but, because these resources are unequally distributed and deployed, some have greater opportunities to influence policy outcomes than others. The state is not a neutral arbiter of social demands or a mirror of society, but neither is it a total partisan of special interests. Nonetheless, it is evident that to govern does mean to choose between differing and competing alternatives. Political choices, involving the regulation of social behaviour, the management of the public sphere and the provision of public services, involve different conceptions of the 'good society'. Such choices are necessarily contested and questioned, but they are temporarily binding, even if they may be changed at some later date. The UK government, like other governments, has a real impact on the functioning of the country and the lives of its citizens – from deciding economic policy and 'getting and spending', to directing reforms in areas such as health, education, transport, social security, the environment and criminal justice policy.

Globalization is often said to undermine government capacity. It is true that in an internationalized world where global capital flows are deemed to limit the autonomy of national policy, power may no longer be the sole preserve of the state (*if* it ever was). Government still, however, retains considerable powers, even though it has to work with and through other actors in the political realm both at home and abroad. For example, in the UK, only government determines issues of war and peace, witnessed most recently in the UK's intervention in Afghanistan and Iraq. Government never take such decisions in social isolation because they are always influenced by public opinion and electoral pressures and by social, economic, diplomatic and geopolitical considerations. Political outcomes are not the sole preserve of the state and its government, but the beliefs and preferences of government actors play a crucial role in prompting policy choices.

In Chapter 1, Richard Heffernan examines the powers and structures of the central state, focusing on the political role of government and parliament. In examining politics at Westminster the chapter looks at executive–legislative relations and intra-executive politics. It demonstrates that, in common with all political systems, the structures of the UK state define and qualify what powers are vested in which central state actors. Heffernan argues that UK politics are characterized by a flexible, amendable constitution, a unitary state and a parliamentary executive able to lead a legislature elected under a single member plurality electoral system. These three factors provide for a centralized government characterized by a strong executive authority.

In Chapter 2, Montserrat Guibernau considers how the nations of England, Wales, Scotland and the contested nation of Northern Ireland came to comprise the United Kingdom. She discusses centre–periphery relations in the UK, contrasting places and spaces where power and resources tend to concentrate (the centre) with other spaces and places which somehow become more marginal (the periphery). In exploring how regional and sub-national politics in the UK either complement or challenge central government, Guibernau analyses the extent to which power and authority has 'passed' from the centre to various peripheries, whether it is going 'outward' to devolved authorities in Scotland and Wales or 'upward' to international actors and institutions such as the European Union. The chapter also discusses how the different political form of a state affects its politics, looking at how unitary and federal and centralized and decentralized states differ one from another.

Several structural features of the UK political system impact on its key political institutions, primarily the government and parliament. These include the single member plurality electoral system, which encourages a party system of at least two main parties and invariably ensures single party government. Chapter 3 by Mads Qvortrup examines the various forms that public participation takes in the UK. The chapter concentrates on electoral processes, particularly the electoral linkages between the state and its citizens, but broadens out to consider other forms of non-systemic participation along with political dissent. It considers how electoral outcomes, public opinion and social movement activity influence government policy, embracing both support for and dissent from the status quo. Qvortrup also examines the opinion-forming role of the UK news media, its impact on electoral politics and its role in policy formation.

The first three chapters, then, concentrate on the more formal processes of politics in the UK. In Chapter 4, Grahame Thompson switches attention to the more informal side of politics and policy making by examining the role and significance of policy networks in the UK. Various forms of policy networks are discussed and the characteristics of their organizational forms explored. Networks are a mechanism by which private interest groups put pressure on governments and help to establish an overall governance framework. Their relationships to corporatism and associationalism are examined and the issues of trust and social capital that they embody discussed. Finally, the relationship between policy networks and other forms of governance, such as hierarchy and the market mechanism, are broached.

In the final chapter, written by Jeremy Mitchell, the broad constitutional reform agenda in the UK is discussed from a particular angle. Following its base in the theme of evidence and argument, Mitchell looks at the different theoretical and ideological frames through which constitutional reform has been viewed in the UK. Politics can be studied from different angles, and Mitchell shows how issues such as constitutional reform throw up different answers depending on how the relevant questions about change are posed. In particular, these issues are explored through questions of the reform proposals for the House of Lords.

In common with all liberal democratic states the UK state does not exercise power over UK society, but works with and through UK society according to the needs and objectives it defines and prioritizes. To this end, like other democratic governments, it seeks the cooperation or co-optation of other social forces. In exploring universal and particular issues in politics, this book uses the UK as a case study. Some studies of comparative politics attempt to explain political phenomena in terms of data collected from across a number of national case studies, but others seek to accumulate and generate a depth and breadth of knowledge about a single subject that broader comparative work cannot hope to match. We adopted the case study approach, therefore, because it enables us to map out the context, contingencies and, indeed, the subtleties of key practices at work in politics and power in the UK.

Governing at the centre: the politics of the parliamentary state

Richard Heffernan

chapter 1

Powers & structures

Contents

1	Introduction	6
2	Government at the centre: the UK's historical political tradition	6
3	How political regimes are organized: presidential/parliamentary and federal/unitary systems	10
4	How political regimes work: majoritarian and consensus democracies	14
5	The political impacts of the flexible and uncodified UK constitution	16
6	Executive–legislative relations within the parliamentary, unitary UK state	21
7	Intra-executive relations within the parliamentary, unitary UK state	26
8	The impacts of the single member plurality electoral system on the parliamentary, unitary UK state	31
9	Conclusion: the UK as an exemplar of a majoritarian democracy	35
	References	39
	Further reading	40

1 INTRODUCTION

A number of actors, among them state officials, electors and citizens, are involved in politics and its policy outcomes. Citizens mostly exercise an indirect or retroactive influence on political life. This is because certain actors have more influence than others, and politics, often a preserve of state officials occupying positions of responsibility, can be largely an elite endeavour. The state, while subject to citizen influence, is granted the power and responsibility to advance policies. As such, the political structures of the state provide the location within which the government of the day operates. Foremost among these structures are the political rules imposed by a constitution. Together, structures and rules determine the practices, boundaries and responsibilities of the government, dictating what is possible for it to do.

Political actors in government are never free agents. They are subject to public opinion and electoral pressures and also have to operate within a prevailing political regime; they must work with, rather than against its grain. Most significantly, liberal democratic states differ in structure according to whether they are presidential or parliamentary, unitary or federal, centralized or decentralized. Such structures complement and constrain the powers of actors who operate within them. As we shall see, governing institutions, political actors, and the public offices they hold (and the relationships between them) are significantly affected by the political regime within which they are located.

2 GOVERNMENT AT THE CENTRE: THE UK'S HISTORICAL POLITICAL TRADITION

The United Kingdom of Great Britain and Northern Ireland (the UK) comprises the nations of England, Wales and Scotland, together with Northern Ireland. As a territory, the UK has external borders recognized both internally and externally. It is a political entity considered legitimate and sovereign by its citizens and by other such states. Its contemporary political form, the political regime through which it governs itself, is the product of a long historical process, one in which a parliamentary system has been slowly fashioned and a liberal democracy established.

History looms large in the making of modern British politics. The UK itself is a union state comprising three historic nations. In 1536, England, having conquered Wales, fused with Wales to form a political entity, and in 1707 a union was forged between England and Wales and Scotland. Scotland, having been in regal union with England since 1603, was thus incorporated into Britain and was governed from Westminster. In 1801, Ireland, long an occupied province of Britain, was also integrated into Britain, but in 1921, 26 Irish counties won independence and left, Northern Ireland remaining in the UK. The island of Ireland was partitioned. Although Britain is an ancient political entity, its roots deep in history, the UK, in its present form at least, is therefore relatively new, dating only from 1922.

The key historical feature in the political governance of the UK has been the governmental role played by a central authority. First, the monarch governed from the capital, London, or wherever he or she was residing. Second, in the modern age, Westminster and Whitehall have been the location of the central authority, the parliamentary government. While there have been institutional differences between the political governance of UK nations (Scotland having distinctive educational, legal and religious institutions), government from the centre has been the rule. As we shall see, however, this has been recently qualified by the UK's membership of the European Union (the EU) and, more marginally, by the introduction of devolution in Scotland and Wales (see Chapter 2). Such recent reforms aside, over time, from the absolutist personal rule of the monarch and his or her court through the emergence of parliamentary rule, Britain has fashioned a centralized, unitary political state. As a result, power has not been institutionally divided between the centre and the locality, even if the centre has worked with and given power to the locality and has been dependent on it to discharge certain policy functions.

The history of the UK tells the tale of the increasing power and authority of parliament. Parliament has been the crucible of two dramatic regime changes over the past four hundred years. First, the eclipse of the monarch as the temporal power in Britain amid the rise of parliament. Second, the rise of an executive, emerging from within parliament, which was eventually to be accountable to the electorate through elections to the House of Commons. As a result, executive power first passed from an absolutist monarchy to a constitutional monarchy governing through parliament. It then passed to parliament itself, and then to a parliamentary executive from within the elected part of the parliament, an executive comprised of leaders able to command a partisan majority of the contemporary parliament. This majority first arose from unelected elite factions formed in parliament, then from elected representatives of political parties.

The historical transformation of the relationship of the executive and the legislature, the Crown and parliament, therefore took the following form:

- an all powerful monarch, anointed to govern by birth and endowed with the divine right to do so, *governed without reference to an advisory parliament*

- a less powerful monarch, obliged to work with economic and political elites beyond the circle of the Crown, *governed through parliament*, the consent of parliament invariably forthcoming out of deference to the Crown

- an increasingly weaker monarch, faced with the consistent erosion of their powers, *governed only with the consent of parliament*, parliament having increasingly wrestled temporal power from the Crown

- the monarch having been stripped of power, a *sovereign parliament governed through the monarch through the government*, the monarch retaining the right to be consulted, to warn and to encourage

- today, *the government, led by the prime minister, governs through parliament without any reference to the ceremonial, non-political monarch*, doing so only nominally in the monarch's name.

Over time the political power of the monarch has dwindled to nothing as parliament gradually asserted all control over the power of the purse (raising and spending monies) and the power of the sword (maintaining law and order and defending the realm). Whereas, say, Henry VIII held the very future of England in his hands every day, Elizabeth II discharges the functions of a ceremonial figurehead. Henry fought wars, made laws, imposed taxes, altered the state religion, executed opponents (and wives), but Elizabeth merely opens events and meets people. The monarch may still, from time to time, be informed about events, but she is no longer consulted, and she probably neither encourages nor warns, as certain constitutional texts suggest (Bagehot, 1963; Bogdanor, 1995).

FIGURE 1.1 The monarch discharging a function of a ceremonial figurehead: the state opening of the UK parliament

In other European settings, in France, Germany, Austria and Italy, monarchies were deposed following social revolution, economic collapse or military defeat. In contrast, over time, Britain gradually and peaceably modernized its restored monarchy into political irrelevance. Although long a stable political unit, Britain did have a political revolution, one born of growing disagreement between monarch and parliament after 1600. This culminated in civil war between 1642 and 1649 in which the Crown was defeated and Charles I executed. This marked the turning point in the power of the monarchy, leading to a less and less powerful monarch, once the monarchy was restored in 1660. Political reforms gradually facilitated the transformation of Britain from an absolutist monarchy into a parliamentary democracy. Yet, as the powers of the Crown, the leadership of the government, passed from the monarch, first to parliament, and then to a parliamentary executive, the government led by the prime minister, it did ensure that a centralist tradition continued. It is this structural feature of UK politics, the empowerment of the centre, which ultimately determines the nature of governmental power. Modern UK politics are characterized by a top down view of democracy often based on the notion that government knows best. It reflects a structural inequality between the centre and the locality, one where the executive – the government of the day – is granted considerable power and authority. As we shall see, this is provided the executive commands the endorsement of parliament and has the support of a plurality of the electorate.

While a centralized state, the UK has never been an authoritarian state. More than most states it has been a study of political stability and an exemplar of political liberalism. This liberal tradition, a mainstay preventing the state from acting in an arbitrary and authoritarian manner, embraces free trade and market exchange, the rule of law, and protects property, contract, individualism and individual rights. In the UK this tradition fostered a constitutionalism which, when gradually married with democracy and the emergence of representative government, more than ensured that government controlled the governed, but also controlled itself. The UK government, however centralized, is not all powerful. For instance, while states as different as Russia, Germany, Spain and Portugal embraced authoritarianism and totalitarianism in the twentieth century, the UK did not. Its centralist politics were limited – checked and balanced by many alternative centres of power, among them civil society, the market economy, the news media, the established church and local government, as well as by centrist, moderate political parties. The centralization of power in the UK has never been accompanied by the accumulation of total power and the abuse of office it promotes.

Centralized power should not then be confused with absolute power. No government, whatever its form, has such power. All liberal democratic governments are subject to any number of checks and balances, foremost among them public opinion, upcoming and anticipated electoral reactions, or news media criticism and interrogation. Governments find themselves unseated if electors do not approve of their record in office or support their political opponents. In addition, government cannot govern alone, having always to work with and through society, so it is dependent on working with sub-national actors (local and regional governments), non-state actors (interest groups and corporate interests) and international actors (the EU, the United Nations and other international organizations). As Grahame Thompson demonstrates in Chapter 4, networks embracing state and non-state actors play a crucial role in governing the country. Corporations, operating locally and globally, clearly influence what government does. In recent years the state has sought to outsource responsibility for service delivery, most notably in privatizing and marketizing a number of public services. Yet, while the state often finds itself dependent on non-state actors for the delivery of services, the UK government retains a unique set of resources – among them legitimacy, law making power, a monopoly of force, an informed and well resourced state bureaucracy, and revenue raising powers through levying taxes – that are unavailable to other actors.

SUMMARY

- The UK government system evolved from an absolutist monarchy to a parliamentary democracy in the context of fashioning a centralized and unitary state.

- The power of parliament is the key to contemporary political authority in the UK.

- A centralized and unitary state does not, however, mean an authoritarian state.

- Nor does centralized power necessarily imply absolute power. There are always checks and balances.

3 HOW POLITICAL REGIMES ARE ORGANIZED: PRESIDENTIAL/PARLIAMENTARY AND FEDERAL/UNITARY SYSTEMS

The territory of a state is governed by the organization of the state, a set of political institutions that provides for the governance of persons and the administration of things. Without such a state, society and civilized life would not be possible. Where the state provides social rules and regulations, liberal democratic constitutionalism provides for citizens' civil and political rights, among them the opportunity to elect the government and the right to personal liberty, privacy, freedom of movement, belief, expression and of association (see **Gieben and Lewis, 2005**). Accountable and democratic government is underpinned by a constitutional order, a set of rules prescribing how the state should be organized. It has four abiding features:

- it is *sovereign* and is the supreme and highest power in the land
- it is *legitimate*, its rule is accepted as correct and proper, and is unchallenged
- it is *authoritative*, the rules it makes being binding, and it has the power to secure compliance with them
- it is *democratic* and citizens are provided with the elective power which helps determine what rules are made and who makes them.

Without these key features, liberal democratic government ceases to be. As such, a constitution has to be supported by the elite and the mass, the ruling and the ruled, by government officials and the citizenry at large.

Governments make and enforce binding rules that are provided for by several political institutions that are involved in the formulation and enactment of laws and public polices. These political institutions are as follows:

- The *constitution* defines the relationship between the state and society, between actors who rule and citizens who are ruled. It also sets out how the state operates, which institutions comprise it and how they relate to one another. It also determines which powers these institutions have and do not have. Constitutions fall into one of two categories: flexible constitutions that can be amended easily and fixed, inflexible constitutions that are difficult to change, being amended only by a super majority.
- The *executive* is the elected government, headed by a prime minister or a president, which recommends and implements rules.
- The *legislature* is the representative elected assembly comprising members of parliament, which makes the rules by enacting laws.
- The *judiciary* is the ultimate legal authority which, depending on the political regime, can adjudicate disputes by enforcing constitutional rules that determine what the executive and the legislature can and cannot do.
- The *electoral system* is the method of converting votes cast in elections into legislative seats that then impact upon executive posts. There are various systems that differ in the degree to which they allocate legislative seats proportionally or disproportionally to the number of votes (see Chapter 3).
- The *party system* describes the number and type of political parties that are engaged in a competitive struggle for electoral support. It also defines the number of parties best placed to seriously compete for sufficient electoral support and actual legislative seats and able to form the government.

Taken together the executive, the legislature and the judiciary form the three key institutions of government. Governments within liberal democracies are elected in a periodic secret ballot of all citizens. Dependent on the political regime, the form of government within which these institutions operate determines the different relationship they will have with one another. We can distinguish four types of political regime in liberal democracies:

- *Presidential systems* directly elect the head of the government, the president, by the people. The president is separate from and autonomous of a separately elected legislature, cannot be removed from office by the legislature, and personally and individually leads and directs the government he or she appoints.

- *Parliamentary systems* indirectly elect the head of the government, the prime minister. The prime minister is not selected by the people, but by the legislature, where the party leader able to command a majority of the legislature becomes prime minister. Being part of and not autonomous of that legislature a prime minister can be removed from office by it, and heads up a collegial government in which other members of the legislature serve under his or her direction.

- *Federal states* are where two or more states constitute a political unity, there are two levels of government, the centre and the locality, the national and the sub-national, and where power is shared between both by the allocation of different political responsibilities to each.

- *Unitary states* are where there is just one level of government, the central government, and where powers are divided between the centre and the locality, the centre deciding what powers are exercised at the locality (see also Chapter 2).

The rules and procedures by which governments operate differ according to the particular form of democracy or political regime. Presidential/parliamentary systems and federal/unitary systems present distinct constitutional arrangements at the governmental centre. They produce very different relationships between the three key branches of government. In particular, the form of government produces very different forms of chief executive, presidents or prime ministers, who are faced with different leadership opportunities and constraints. Table 1.1 gives examples of different political regimes.

TABLE 1.1   Examples of presidential/parliamentary and federal/unitary political systems

	Federal	Unitary
Presidential	United States of America	France (semi-presidential, with a directly elected president, but an executive drawn from the legislature headed by a prime minister)
Parliamentary	Germany, Australia	United Kingdom, Republic of Ireland

Presidential/parliamentary systems and federal/unitary systems can helpfully be seen as part of a broader distinction between two types of liberal democracy: *majoritarian* and *consensus* democracies (Lijphart, 1984, 1999). As discussed in the next section, these are defined as follows:

- A majoritarian democracy places power in the hands of a majority (and often a plurality, a majority over all other minorities, but not all minorities together, nor an overall majority), and centralizes decision making.

- A consensus democracy aims to empower a majority as a minimum and share, disperse and limit power in a variety of institutional ways.

Political systems determine the system of government. How do they decide

> who will do the governing and to whose interests should the government be responsive when the people are in disagreement and have divergent preferences? One answer to this dilemma is: the majority of the people. This is the essence of the majoritarian model of democracy ... . The alternative answer to the dilemma is: as many people as possible. This is the crux of the consensus model.
>
> (Lijphart, 1999, pp.1–2)

The powers and structures that exist in a liberal democracy, the political institutions that help provide for the governance of persons and the administration of things, therefore express either the majoritarian or the consensus model of democracy.

SUMMARY

- Accountable and democratic government is underpinned by a *constitutional order* involving the following features: it must be sovereign, legitimate, authoritative and democratic.

- Liberal democratic *political institutions of government* comprise a constitution, an executive, a legislature, a judiciary, an electoral system and a party system.

- *Political regimes* in liberal democracies can be either presidential or parliamentary and involving either federal or unitary state forms.

- There are two basic *types of liberal democracies*, majoritarian or consensus.

4 HOW POLITICAL REGIMES WORK: MAJORITARIAN AND CONSENSUS DEMOCRACIES

The UK executive governs subject to the usual democratic checks and balances, provided it commands the support of the legislature elected at a general election. Table 1.2 illustrates the basic differences between majoritarian and consensus democracies.

TABLE 1.2   The Lijphart model: distinguishing majoritarian and consensus democracies

	Majoritarian	Consensus
Form of government	Unitary and centralized.	Federal and decentralized.
Legislative structure	Concentration of legislative power in a unicameral legislature or in one chamber of a two chamber legislature.	Legislative power shared between two equally strong but differently constituted legislative chambers.
Constitutional form	Flexible constitutions that can be amended by simple majority.	Rigid fixed constitutions that can be changed only by extraordinary majority.
Judicial review	Legislatures have the final word on the constitutionality of their own legislation.	Laws are subject to a judicial review of their constitutionality by supreme or constitutional courts.
Executive government	Concentration of executive power in single party government.	Executive power sharing in broad multi-party coalitions.
Executive–legislative relations	Executive–legislative relations in which the executive is dominant.	Executive–legislative balance.
Electoral system	Majoritarian and disproportional electoral system.	Proportional representation.
Party system	Two party system.	Multi-party system.

National political systems can be located somewhere on a continuum between the two types of democracies with majoritarian democracies at one end, consensus democracies at the other. No particular system will embody all the features. The UK is, with key exceptions, close to the ideal type majoritarian model. Historically, while local governments have been granted certain powers by the centre, there has been little dispersion of power between the centre and the locality in the UK. Since 1997 Scottish and Welsh devolution has clearly made the unitary, centralized state less unitary, less centralized. Some argue that devolution has made the UK a quasi-federal system (Bogdanor, 2003), but this suggestion is contested, particularly as devolved authorities govern only 15 per cent of UK citizens living in Scotland and Wales; 85 per cent live in England and are still wholly governed by the centre, the Westminster parliament.

More importantly, thanks to its membership of the EU, the UK shares competences with Europe in a number of policy areas (see Chapter 2). In regard to trade, industrial and competition policy, agricultural policy, environmental protection, it is EU policy, agreed under international treaties, that affects what happens in the UK. Clearly, under all forms of government, no central government can (or would wish to) do everything. Delegation to local government and the pooling of certain sovereignties at the European level reflects the fact that political realities, economic need and international commitments require even the most powerful centre to share power with other actors. The majoritarian model does not suggest that all power is centralized, only much of it, suggesting that powers which are delegated elsewhere may, in theory at least, be reclaimed.

As we shall see, the UK's unified parliamentary government facilitates the fusion of the executive (the government) and the legislature (parliament). It also provides for legislative predominance over the judiciary. UK politics are primarily conducted between the executive and the legislative branches, against the ever-present important backdrop of public opinion and electoral outcomes (Chapter 3). The judicial branch is formally 'non-political' (even if judges have their own personal political preferences). Its role is largely confined to implementing whatever legislation is passed by parliament, but the judiciary can interpret the meaning of parliamentary law when it is vague or where one law conflicts with other laws. Judges have the right to interpret the expressed or implied intent of parliament and can sometimes decide whether ministers exceed the powers granted them by parliament, but they do not make or change law. While providing for legislative predominance over the judiciary, the UK model of democracy facilitates executive dominance over the legislature. The UK's parliamentary system and its electoral system, the single member plurality system (SMPS), usually ensure that the executive takes the form of a single party government. As a disproportional electoral system SMPS facilitates a two party system in terms of party alternation in government.

In sharp contrast, because the USA is a presidential, federal system, it divides power vertically (within the central federal government) and horizontally (between the federal government and the 50 states of the union). The US government is based on separated, shared powers between the executive, the legislature and the judiciary. Each institution is separately constituted by different arrangements: separate election in the case of the president; separate election for the two different houses of Congress, the House of Representatives and the Senate; and presidential nomination with legislative approval in the case of the Supreme Court. In addition, the USA has a limited government governed by an inflexible constitution. Laws passed by the president and the Congress (and by the state governments) are subject to judicial review, their constitutionality determined by federal courts and a constitutional court, the Supreme Court. The judiciary has the power to strike down legislation or public actions that are not provided for in the US constitution. The USA is a consensus democracy, but has some majoritarian features built in, among them a single party government, a two party system and a plurality rule electoral system. The USA remains, when compared with the UK, a more decentralized political entity.

Centralization is the name of the political game in the UK; decentralization, for the most part, except for occasions of national emergency and issues of national security, defence and foreign policy, is the ballpark theme in the USA. Such different political structures provide very different powers for the UK and US governments.

SUMMARY

- 'Majoritarian' and 'consensus' are ideal types of democratic political systems. They exist on a continuum, no actual system demonstrates every feature.

- The UK model is closer to the majoritarian end of the spectrum, fusing the legislature with the executive, invariably empowering the executive, with both prevailing over the judiciary.

- The USA is closer to the consensus end of the spectrum, but with strong built-in majoritarian features.

5 THE POLITICAL IMPACTS OF THE FLEXIBLE AND UNCODIFIED UK CONSTITUTION

The UK has one of the oldest parliaments in the world, but modern UK democracy, defined as one-person-one-vote in parliamentary elections at the age of 18, dates only from 1970. Hence, democracy, defined as the right to choose one's Member of Parliament, has only a very recent history. In 1831 only 1.8 per cent of the adult population, all men, were eligible to vote. In 1832, thanks to The Great Reform Act, the franchise was extended to 2.7 per cent of the population, all still male. In 1867 the franchise was extended to some 6.4 per cent of the male population, which then increased to 12 per cent in 1884. Only in 1918 were working class men and women over the age of 30 finally enfranchised. Full and equal adult suffrage, one-person-one-vote at the age of 21, was finally secured in 1928, the franchise then being lowered to 18 in 1970.

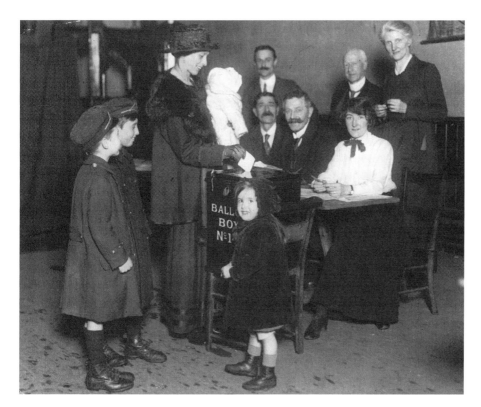

FIGURE 1.2   An enfranchised woman votes for the first time in the UK

Of course, the UK was not alone in this grudging extension of democratic rights. Indeed, excepting past attitudes to women's suffrage, it could make claim to be better than most. Women did not have voting rights in the USA until 1920, France 1944 and Switzerland 1971. The USA only firmly established universal suffrage in all 50 states of the union with the passage of the 1965 Civil Rights Act that finally outlawed all residual racial discrimination in voting. In Australia, Aborigines could not vote until 1962.

In all cases, the extensions of the franchise (and its limitation) were constitutional decisions. Democratic constitutions not only prescribe what the state can and cannot do vis-à-vis society, they also determine how (and if) citizens can elect the government. In this regard, constitutional structures decided who could and could not vote, empowering certain citizens while limiting others. Prevailing political structures thereby determine how citizens may hold government to account for its actions or otherwise influence what the state does. As importantly, however, constitutions also map out and define the interrelationship between the key institutions that comprise the state, primarily the executive and the legislature. The UK constitution therefore provides the key structure within which UK politics are transacted, defining the rules by which the UK state operates. It has two primary features:

- it is uncodified, rather than codified, that is, it is not written down in any one particular place, or found in one legal document
- it is flexible, rather than fixed.

Modern constitutions, invariably the product of pre-planned preparation where a constitution is designed from scratch, have been the norm since the late eighteenth century. This reflects the Enlightenment experience, when, building on the work of theorists such as Locke, Montesquieu and others, it was prescribed that constitutions should be written, codified legal documents, available and understandable to all. In each national case, constitution making was the product of national historical experiences, but modern constitutions were mostly enacted when the previous constitutional arrangements collapsed, usually due to extensive social dislocation, either as a result of defeat in war, occupation and/or liberation, or of social revolution. Three examples of modern constitutions forged as the result of social upheaval are the constitutions of:

- the United States of America (prompted by social revolution and the winning of independence from Britain, 1775–1787)
- Japan (prompted by defeat in war and occupation, 1945–49)
- Germany (prompted by defeat in war and occupation, 1945–49).

Between 1789 and 1945 social upheavals in France saw the rise and fall of two monarchies, two empires, five republics and one proto-fascist dictatorship. Germany had four separate constitutions in the twentieth century alone. Each time the constitution changed because the old order collapsed: in 1919, as a result of defeat in war and social revolution; in 1933, due to political revolution by way of the Nazi seizure of power; and after 1945, following the destruction of the Third Reich, the occupation of Germany by the four Allied Powers (the USA, the UK, the Soviet Union and France) and its division into East and West.

Many constitutions can be interpreted, but are not easily changed. In contrast, the UK constitution can easily change. Because there is no single moment of settlement, as, say, in the USA in 1787 or Germany in 1919 or 1949, the UK constitution has changed slowly, being moulded incrementally to changing circumstances. Unlike other constitutions which are written down, listing rules and regulations in one codified legally binding document, the UK's constitution is uncodified. Whereas the founding fathers met in Philadelphia in 1787 to design the US constitution, the UK constitution was never designed by any one group of individuals, meeting in any one place at any one time. Having abandoned the previous constitutional order by securing independence from Britain, the founders of the USA had to construct a new constitution. While the US constitution was written down in a single document, an original of which, signed by the delegates to the Constitutional Convention, may be viewed in the National Archives in Washington DC, the UK constitution does not exist in such a form. It is found in several places, not in any single legal document, and is comprised of five very diverse sources, shown in Table 1.3.

TABLE 1.3   Five sources of the UK constitution

Statute law	Acts passed by parliament.
Common law	Law unaffected by statute and prescribed by the judiciary where parliament has not made any ruling by enacting legislation.
Custom and practice	Well established rules of procedure and precedent to which all are expected to comply.
Authoritative and scholarly works	Works written as attempts by scholars to semi-codify the constitution and define its rules, such as Erskine May's *Parliamentary Practice* (first published in 1844 and updated numerous times since then), Walter Bagehot's *The English Constitution* (1867) and, most famous of all, Dicey's *Introduction to the Study of the Law of the Constitution* (1885).
European law and accession treaties	A series of international agreements to which the UK has signed up to since 1973 (by 2004: the Treaties of Rome, Maastricht, Amsterdam and Nice and the Single European Act) and which now determine what government can and cannot do in a number of policy arenas.

These five sources of constitutional law in the UK mean that the UK constitution is to be found on the various shelves of an academic library, not hung on the wall of a national museum. UK constitutional practice is the product of an historical experience, laws, customs and conventions being added to and subtracted from over time as circumstances dictate. This is because the UK constitution is *flexible*, rather than fixed. Of the above sources of constitutional law statute law is now the most important constitutional source. New statute law supersedes all other considerations. Because the *sovereignty of parliament* is at the heart of UK constitutional practice parliament can make and unmake any constitutional law it wishes; no act it passes can be unconstitutional. 'No person or body is recognized by the law of England [*sic*] as having a right to override or set aside the legislation of parliament' (Dicey, 1959, p.40). *Government in the UK is predicated upon the rule of law and parliament has the unfettered right to make the law.* There is no higher national authority than parliament, so no other institution may regulate its actions except electors who can retrospectively judge its decisions and alter its political composition at a subsequent election. Since 1973, however, parliament has voluntarily qualified this in regard to policies that fall under the rubric of the EU. Here it is accepted that, where there is a conflict between the two, EU law takes precedence over domestic law. However, the UK parliament has pooled, not necessarily surrendered its sovereignty. While practical considerations, the need to be within Europe for economic reasons, might well make withdrawal from the EU problematic, the UK is constitutionally free to leave the EU should it so wish.

In the USA, a constitutional court, the Supreme Court, can strike down decisions of the president and the Congress it deems unconstitutional. In the UK, there is no such judicial review because there is no higher constitutional standard by which parliament is judged. Unlike the US Congress, the UK parliament regulates itself. Within it, all power lies, and such powers not found in parliament have been delegated by parliament to other bodies such as the EU, the Scottish Parliament and the National Assembly for Wales. There is, therefore, no procedure to render a parliamentary act unconstitutional: by their very nature, all parliamentary acts are constitutional. While parliament is in theory free to do whatever it likes, in practice it is restrained by what MPs allow, citizens ultimately permit, and practical politics deem possible.

As such, the UK constitution, for want of a better metaphor, is a reworked patchwork quilt, added to and subtracted from when deemed necessary by parliament. It is amended by the enactment of a parliamentary bill, because the UK parliament, able to pass any bill it chooses, can make and unmake any law, even as it binds its own hands in regard to EU competences. By altering statute law it may change the constitution at any time. However, no parliament can bind its successor.

While the UK constitution is easily changed, it is only changed by a parliamentary majority, most usually in response to pressing, urgent public demands, or perceived national need. For instance, the constitution was incrementally altered between 1832 and 1970 to gradually extend the electoral franchise for the House of Commons to all adults irrespective of class or gender. Parliament whittled the power of the monarch down to nothing and oversaw the UK's divestment of its far-flung empire. Most recently, although there has been little historical dispersion of power between the centre and the locality, the Labour government legislated to create Scottish and Welsh devolution (see Chapter 2). It did so because Labour Party policy willed it: Labour was elected in 1997 on a manifesto commitment to proceed with devolution, and the citizens of those nations demanded it by referendum. The constitution has been altered organically because being flexible, it is easily amendable: constitutional reform, whatever other motivations might lay behind it, is ultimately facilitated by majoritarian politics, the will of the majority in parliament (whatever checks and balances might be brought to bear upon them) even if sometimes prompted by other factors.

SUMMARY

- While the USA has a limited government, the UK has an unlimited government.

- The political system of the USA is predicated upon a fixed, inflexible constitution, whereas the UK has a strong, authoritative government empowered by a fluid, flexible constitution.

- The primary political impact of the UK constitution is to empower parliament and grant authority to the government able to command a majority within that parliament.

6 EXECUTIVE–LEGISLATIVE RELATIONS WITHIN THE PARLIAMENTARY, UNITARY UK STATE

Executive–legislative relations differ according to whether a liberal democracy is a presidential or a parliamentary system or a federal or a unitary state. In the UK, as we have seen, the judiciary does not have the power to regulate the decisions of the government endorsed by parliament, so judges play little part in influencing the political life of the nation. The structured relationship between the UK executive, known as the government or as Whitehall, and the legislature, also known as parliament or as Westminster, lies at the heart of the working of UK parliamentary politics. Most importantly, because the UK constitution empowers the legislature by making it alone responsible for constitutional reform, it actually serves to empower the legislative majority, the executive, with that power of reform.

As with the UK constitution, the UK parliament is a product of its historical background. From the thirteenth century on, parliament was conceived in the practice of the monarch to summon powerful representatives from territorial localities to help him or her govern. Representatives administered the locality on behalf of the centre, rendering advice as to policy, and raised money, men and material to protect and extend the realm. As such, the present day UK parliament still resembles the historical parliament, but only in structure. Its powers have altered radically as the organic constitution has been altered to embrace modern realities. There are still three formal parts of the UK legislature:

- the Monarch, the official, albeit now wholly ceremonial Head of State

- the House of Lords, the 'upper' house of parliament

- the House of Commons, the 'lower' house of parliament.

Distinguishing between what Walter Bagehot termed the efficient and the dignified parts of the constitution, the useful and the ceremonial (Bagehot, 1963) is a helpful way of distinguishing UK institutions. The monarch is now merely a dignified part of the political system and does not have any efficient power. Only the Commons and the Lords legislate and, while the monarch still has to sign bills into law, constitutional convention dictates they do so automatically. Thus the UK parliament is a *bicameral parliament*, in that there are two legislative chambers. However, while the House of Commons and the House of Lords both have to process legislation, they are profoundly unequal, so the UK parliament is *asymmetrically bicameral* (Lijphart, 1999). The Lords is only a weak, reactive, revising chamber. Where once the Lords and Commons were equal in legislative power, an example of symmetrical bicameralism, they are no longer (Norton, 1993). The Commons, which became the elected chamber as the voting franchise expanded, accrued power at the expense of the unelected, hereditary Lords, a chamber that came to be seen as an anachronism, associated with the past, not the present. However, there is a lively debate about the reform of the House of Lords which is reviewed by Jeremy Mitchell in Chapter 5. The membership and functions of the two houses as of early 2004 are outlined in Tables 1.4 and 1.5.

TABLE 1.4   Membership and functions of the House of Lords

Membership	Unelected, its members are not necessarily professional politicians. Until 1999 it was composed of two types of member, known as peers: life peers, appointed by successive prime ministers, and hereditary peers. Hereditary peers, created by past prime ministers and monarchs, were able to pass their membership down through their male line until 1999 when hereditary peerages were abolished. In 2004, the Lords was composed of some 583 life peers, 92 former hereditary peers now converted into life peers, and 26 bishops of the established church, the Church of England.
Relationship with the government	Provides only a handful of junior ministers and usually two members of the Cabinet.
Legislative function	Subordinate to the House of Commons. It may revise legislation presented to it by the Commons, but may not insist on the amendments it makes. By so insisting it may delay the passage of legislation, but only for one year whereupon the House of Commons may then enact the bill in question without reference to the Lords. The Lords is not permitted to discuss financial bills.

TABLE I.5   Membership and functions of the House of Commons

Membership	It is composed of 659 elected MPs representing similarly sized single member constituencies.
Relationship with the government	The House of Commons provides all but a handful of members of the government and all senior ministers. It decides which party forms the government on the basis of a simple partisan majority. If Labour secures more MPs than all other parties combined, Labour will form the government. There is no separation of power between the legislature and the executive. All senior ministers, foremost among them the prime minister, have to sit in the Commons. The government is formed based on the distribution of Commons seats usually following a general election.
Legislative function	It has prime legislative competence (although it grants precedence to EU legislation) and can override decisions of the House of Lords beyond a one year delay.

The key function of the UK legislature is to provide the UK executive. Where the US executive, in the person of the president, is elected directly and independently of the Congress, the UK executive is elected indirectly and emerges from the elected part of the legislature, the House of Commons. Citizens only indirectly elect the government by granting a Commons majority to one particular party. No elector voted for Tony Blair to be prime minister in 1997 or 2001, electors only elected an MP to represent the constituency in which they live, one of 659 constituencies in the whole of the UK. When sufficient Labour MPs were elected to form a Commons majority, Tony Blair became prime minister.

The executive, formed and led by a prime minister, is dependent on the Commons but, as we shall see, the relationship between the government and the House of Commons is an unequal one. Provided it is able to command a parliamentary majority, the government is able to dominate parliament. The larger the parliamentary majority, the stronger the government; the smaller the majority, the weaker the government. The non-separation of powers between the executive and the legislature, the government and the parliament, is the very keystone of the UK's parliamentary system. As a result, the UK is one of two types of liberal democratic legislature. These two types can be distinguished as follows.

- A policy-making legislature which has the power to enact laws and is a legislature that can modify or reject measures brought forward by the executive and can formulate and substitute policies of its own. The US legislature, the Congress, elected separately from and independent of the US executive, the presidency, falls quite clearly into this category.

FIGURE 1.3   The modern Palace of Westminster, once the seat of monarchical power but now the national forum that grants power to government

- A policy-influencing legislature which has the power to enact laws and is a legislature that can modify or reject measures brought forward by the executive but cannot formulate and substitute policies of its own.

The first category, the policy-making legislature, is a *proactive* legislature. The second category is a *reactive* legislature. The UK parliament is a *policy-influencing* legislature, and it is most certainly *reactive* in nature. It should also be remembered that the overall *policy-making process* in a country such as the UK is the result of a number of different determinations and levels, and not simply a parliamentary activity (see Chapter 4 and **Prokhovnik, 2005**).

Following an election the party with the majority of MPs has the right to form the government. That government is able to have parliament pass its legislation because of the backing of a partisan majority. This is the power the political structure of the UK grants the government. Without the support of a majority of the House of Commons, the government would cease to be. With that support, the government can pass its legislation. This is provided, of course, it has, as it invariably does, its own MPs onside. Walter Bagehot once claimed that 'The efficient secret of the English Constitution may be described as the close union, the nearly complete fusion, of the legislative and executive powers ... We are ruled by the House of Commons' (Bagehot, 1963, p.65). Today, however, rather than being ruled by the Commons, the UK is in fact ruled by a government able to act through the House of Commons. This is because the House of Commons has two conflicting primary functions within the UK political system:

- providing and supporting the government, enacting legislation it presents, and supporting the government's continuation in office
- overseeing the work of the government, scrutinizing its activity, and holding it to account for what it does.

These primary functions, the very product of the non-separation of powers between government and parliament, conflict with one another. They conflict because the Commons majority provides the government of the day. As a result, this partisan majority provides and supports the government. In supporting the government in office, parliament cannot easily check and balance the government's activities. For the most part, the majority party has little interest in doing so, preferring to enact the government's legislative programme and, as critics suggest, cheerlead for it.

Parliamentary scrutiny is affected by the partisan nature of parliament itself. For the most part, government MPs support the government, even if they grumble and complain about it. Rebellions do take place, but they are the exceptions, not the rule. Opposition MPs usually oppose the government, even if they may privately agree with what it is doing. All MPs are elected as representatives of their political party: seats are won by parties, not by individual candidates, so by using carrot or stick governments can persuade their MPs to follow the line. Patronage, the ability of the prime minister to reward MPs with government jobs, is often the glue that binds the government together. The prime minister appoints ministers to the government from among his or her party's MPs. Government backbenchers, aware that backbench loyalty is the best way to work a ministerial ticket from the prime minister, may often be eager to secure preferment by supporting the party line. However, they might also support the government because they agree with its policy. Government MPs do not always support the government merely out of ambition and self interest; many do so out of the conviction that the government's policy is correct and it is what their party has a right to expect from them. Nonetheless, partisanship, the obligation MPs feel to be supportive rather than critical of their party government, runs deep. As a nineteenth century prime minister, Benjamin Disraeli, once famously advised an aspirant politician, 'damn your principles and stick to your party'. This writ runs large in the modern House of Commons.

Free in theory, given its partisan majority, to *command* the legislature, the executive finds it can in practice only *lead* it. Reliant on its own backbenchers to enact its legislation, the government cannot always assume they will always support its proposals unquestioningly, whether out of conviction or expediency. The

FIGURE 1.4   The gateway to Whitehall, the actual seat of government

government does require its MPs to toe its legislative line, and is able to persuade them to do so by appeals to loyalty, promotion and threats of punishment. In practice, *a law of anticipated reactions* can limit the power of government to automatically lead parliament. While weak, parliament is not always a 'rubber stamp' that endorses the policy of the government. MPs will not always reply 'how high' when a prime minister asks them to jump. While able to rely on backbench goodwill, governments and prime ministers are aware that they cannot endlessly dragoon reluctant MPs into the government division lobby for fear of encouraging resentment, so storing up trouble for the future; even the most emollient worm may one day turn.

This is why, however weak and reactive a legislature the UK parliament may be, it should not be seen as a toothless tiger. In theory, it is one of the most powerful legislatures in the world, able to make and break governments at will, dismissing them from office by a vote of no confidence. However, although a sharp-toothed tiger, it is one that rarely chooses to bite, a tiger muzzled as it were by partisan politics, in this case the willingness of the majority party to support its government through thick and thin, in good times and bad. Being able to lead the legislature is therefore a valued resource of the UK executive.

SUMMARY

- The UK is an asymmetrical bicameral parliamentary system.
- The key function of its legislature is to provide the personnel for the executive.
- The government of the day is invariably able to dominate parliament, provided it has a partisan majority.
- The UK parliament is a reactive, policy-influencing legislature.
- By and large, MPs support their party and their government, and can sometimes do so against their better judgement.

7 INTRA-EXECUTIVE RELATIONS WITHIN THE PARLIAMENTARY, UNITARY UK STATE

The UK executive comprises elected ministers drawn from the legislature, foremost among them the prime minister, together with unelected permanent civil servants, bureaucrats who work under the direction of ministers. With the exception of the prime minister, ministers and civil servants are organized within departments, and are charged with implementing policy in specific areas. The prime minister, the parliamentary chief executive, is the head of the government, responsible for the appointment of ministers, setting the government's policy agenda, and providing general oversight of its policy deliberations (Hennessy, 2000). While the Queen is the nominal head of state, the prime minister is the actual head of state in all but name. Under the UK constitution, the prime minister has, by convention, not law, to have three formal practical qualifications to occupy the post, these being:

- an elected member of the House of Commons

- the leader of a political party represented in the House of Commons

- the leader of the political party with an overall majority in the House of Commons (or leader of the largest minority political party able to command a Commons majority either in coalition with one or more political parties or as a single party government because other parties will not combine to pass a vote of no confidence).

All prime ministers since Lord Salisbury, who retired in 1902, have been members of the House of Commons. It is no longer possible for a peer, a member of the House of Lords, to become prime minister. The last peer to do so, Alec Douglas-Home, had to resign from the Lords and win election to the Commons to succeed Harold Macmillan in 1963. Tony Blair, at the time of writing, is the only individual to hold the three formal job qualifications noted above. He is an MP, as Labour MP for Sedgefield since 1983; a party leader, as leader of the Labour Party since July 1994; and because Labour won the 1997 and 2001 general elections he has been leader of the majority party in the House of Commons since May 1997.

The structural imperatives of the UK's parliamentary system determine the relationship of the executive and the legislature and decide the powers of the prime minister. As the head of the government the prime minister is 'first among equals'.

- He or she is 'first' because prime ministers appoint and dismiss ministers, allocate and reallocate portfolios, and manage the Cabinet and the Cabinet system. He or she delegates powers to other ministers, but must be consulted, either directly or indirectly, about all significant matters relating to government policy. Such powers place the prime minister at the centre of key executive networks, with the capacity to exert a significant influence on the policy agenda and over the government machine.

- He or she is 'among equals' because the government is composed of semi-autonomous political actors drawn from the legislature, each of which could replace the prime minister as head of the government.

FIGURE 1.5 Tony Blair after winning the general election, June 2001: as an MP, party leader and leader of the winning party he holds the three formal job qualifications to be prime minister

Some suggest that the modern prime minister has become so powerful that he or she is essentially a 'president' (Foley, 2000). Such criticism, while focusing on the reality of prime ministerial power, misunderstands the nature of the premiership. The three qualifications for being prime minister listed above provide the tripod upon which the prime minister stands. Should these qualifications be lost, no prime ministerial actor can retain the post. In May 1997, Tony Blair's predecessor, John Major, ceased to be prime minister when the Conservatives' general election defeat meant his party no longer had an overall Commons majority. In November 1990, Major had replaced Margaret Thatcher when, having lost the confidence of MPs and ministers, she resigned as leader of the Conservative Party. Thatcher resigned even though her party retained a handsome Commons majority.

The prime minister is not a president, because presidents cannot usually be removed by their legislature. Indeed, prime ministers are necessarily more powerful than presidents, particularly when, such as the UK prime minister, they are located within a majoritarian democracy. They automatically possess coterminous executive and legislative majorities, even as they require such majorities to retain their office. While they exist, such majorities provide prime ministers with power. Presidents, by contrast, are never able to lead their separately elected and autonomous legislatures in ways prime ministers can. They are faced with far more checks, balances and veto powers. Prime ministers lead their government by heading up a *collegial* executive, but presidents, being directly elected in their own right, head up an *individual* executive. US presidential administrations are composed of non-autonomous actors who cannot replace the directly elected president. Unlike all US Cabinet members, senior UK Cabinet ministers (by no means all of them) can have an independent political base of their own which makes them an independent colleague of, not a subordinate agent to, the prime minister.

Of course, all heads of government, be they prime minister or president, have power but have also to work with and through other governmental actors. They share as well as exercise power, have to delegate authority, win the support (or avoid the disapproval) of powerful interests, appease key electorates, communicate policies, and negotiate all sorts of political and economic obstacles. In having to react to crises or respond to problems, prime ministers find they are as reactive as they are proactive.

Within the hierarchy of the UK's central government, however, while a government can be very powerful, the prime minister may be important, but he or she is never all important, nor ever all powerful. Constraints such as time, knowledge, expertise and the sheer number of issues modern government has to process means prime ministers have to work with and through their ministers. While theoretically free to appoint any MP to any position, in practice, prime ministers have to reward friends and appease could-be rivals. They wisely apply the crude principle enunciated by US President Lyndon Johnson, namely keeping potential rivals 'inside the leadership tent pissing out', rather than having them 'outside the tent pissing in'. This is because power does 'vary from Prime Minister to Prime Minister, and ... according to the political strength that a particular Prime Minister has at any given time' (Lawson, 1994, p.441). The prime minister's power is not permanent, may well be transitory, and certainly alters over time. The UK political system does not automatically create a powerful prime minister, although a powerful prime minister such as Tony Blair or Margaret Thatcher may dominate government for considerable periods. The prime minister requires two key power resources to operate effectively:

- authority within the executive
- predominance over the legislature.

A prime minister is ultimately dependent on their party within the House of Commons for their office, hence demonstrating the great importance of the parliamentary structures within which he or she obtains office. In practice, a Labour majority in the Commons would not vote to remove a Labour government; nor would a Conservative majority remove a Conservative government. However, in theory, the executive does not have a secure tenure in office, because it can be removed at any time. As we have seen, if the government does not change, then the prime minister might, as in the case of Mrs Thatcher in 1990. In contrast, the directly elected US president, unlike the indirectly elected UK prime minister, being separate from and independent of the US legislature, does have a secure tenure. The US Congress cannot remove him or her, save by impeachment, a process reserved as a response to 'high crimes and misdemeanours'. This has only been attempted twice, most recently in the impeachment of Bill Clinton in 1998–99, but has never been successfully implemented, although in 1974 the 37th President, Richard Nixon, did resign before he could be impeached. In Table 1.6 (overleaf) the features of UK prime ministers and US presidents are compared.

To govern, prime ministers have to be able to lead their executive, set the policy agenda, and command the loyalty of their ministers. Here, a key resource available to the prime minister is their leadership of a unitary, centralized and disciplined parliamentary party, particularly when a governing party cares little about the legislature's role as a check and balance on the executive. In structural terms there is no separation of power between the UK executive (headed by the majority party leader as prime minister) and the UK legislature (headed by the prime minister as majority party leader). It is this structural imperative that enables a prime minister to form and maintain the executive and for that executive to have the opportunity to formulate and implement its policy agenda.

SUMMARY

- The UK prime minister can be very powerful, but is not all powerful.
- The prime minister is not like a US president. Their powers differ.
- All prime ministers head up a collegial executive, one within which power is shared, to some extent, between the prime minister and other ministers.

TABLE 1.6   Comparing and contrasting the UK prime minister with the US president

	Prime minister	President
Elected directly by a national vote	No.	Yes.
Has to be a member of the legislature	Yes. Has to be a member of the House of Commons.	No. Cannot be a member of the legislature due to a strict separation of powers between executive and legislature.
Placed in office by legislative majority	Yes. Emerges from the House of Commons, is wholly dependent on party majority and accountable to it.	No. Elected separately and independently of legislature.
Can be removed by a simple vote of the legislature for political reasons	Yes. Or be removed from the party leadership by his or her own MPs.	No. May only be impeached for 'high crimes and misdemeanours' for which a super legislative majority is required.
Term limited	No. Can serve for so long as their party permits them to remain in office or their party retains a Commons majority.	Yes. Can only be re-elected once, serving two four-year terms in total.
Executive form	Collegial. Being 'first among equals' the prime minister appoints ministers and leads the government. Ministers, particularly senior ministers, being politicians in their own right, work with but may not necessarily be instructed by the prime minister. All ministers may replace the prime minister, provided they obtain the support of the parliamentary party to do so.	Individualized. Cabinet members have to report to the president and, while able to confer advice, must follow his or her preferred policies. No member of the executive can replace the president, save the vice-president should the president be incapacitated, resign or be impeached.

8 THE IMPACTS OF THE SINGLE MEMBER PLURALITY ELECTORAL SYSTEM ON THE PARLIAMENTARY, UNITARY UK STATE

Political parties link citizens to political institutions and facilitate representative government, determining which actors hold what legislative and executive posts at national, regional and local levels. Now, perhaps more than ever, parties are dominated by powerful and predominant leaderships. This leadership, the party in 'public office', has become the key feature of contemporary party politics. Parties now: have smaller memberships and a very low voter/member ratio; are orientated toward 'opinion electorates' rather than traditional voters, their 'electorate of belonging'; emphasize issues or personalities rather than ideology; and are increasingly reliant on corporations, wealthy individuals or government for financial support (see Chapter 3). The parliamentary party, the party at Westminster, has become ever more important than the party at large in the country.

As the buckle linking electors to government, parties stand or fall on their electoral performance. Winning votes and gaining public office is one objective; running the country in line with their ideological and policy preferences another. Prime ministers or opposition leaders who do not deliver such valued goods to their parliamentary parties may find they lose support and may in time forfeit their jobs.

Election outcomes are dependent on the electoral system that converts votes cast into seats won. Winning votes at general elections is different from winning legislative seats. Different electoral systems produce different electoral outcomes. As we have seen, majoritarian democracies use disproportional electoral systems and consensus democracies proportional electoral systems. The UK has a single member plurality system (SMPS), sometimes called first past the post, the most disproportional electoral system of all. Under SMPS the winning candidate in each constituency need only poll more votes than his or her nearest rival (see Chapter 3 and **Smith, 2005**). In a hypothetical example, should the vote split 33–33–34 per cent in a three way contest, the candidate with 34 per cent of the vote will win the seat, even though 66 per cent of the electorate did not vote for him or her. If that result were repeated across all constituencies, then one party would win all the seats on 34 per cent of the vote: here, 34 per cent of the vote would equate to 100 per cent of the legislative seats.

SMPS does not ensure any necessary correlation between votes won and seats gained, but only gives seats to the party with a plurality of the vote. Proportional representation (PR) systems, whichever one is used, produce a more proportional relationship between votes and seats. This does not happen under SMPS, where vote and seat share need not correlate, as is illustrated in Table 1.7.

TABLE 1.7 Relationship between share of vote and share of seats under SMPS at the 2001 general election

	Percentage share of the vote	Percentage share of the seats in the House of Commons
Labour	42	64
Conservative	33	26
Liberal Democrats	19	8

Institutional rules help determine political outcomes. SMPS grants legislative majorities to the largest electoral plurality, usually a minority. Such is the effect of SMPS, if the House of Commons were elected by a PR electoral system, the Labour Party would not have won a three figure seat majority in 1997 or 2001. The party would then most likely have had to form a coalition government with the third party, the Liberal Democrats. Under SMPS, in 2001 42 per cent of the vote gave Labour 64 per cent of Commons seats, when 58 per cent of those voting voted against Labour (and when a turn-out of 59 per cent meant approximately 75 per cent of the total electorate did not vote Labour). SMPS encourages *single party government*, obviating the need for coalition, multi-party government. This phenomenon forms a key part of the UK's majoritarian political structure. No political party has ever secured over 50 per cent of the vote in the post-Second World War period, but in this period, excepting February to October 1974 when Labour formed a minority government, 1977–79 when James Callaghan led another minority Labour government (and John Major in the dog days of the 1997 parliament), all governments have had more than 50 per cent of the seats in the House of Commons. Many governments have had over 60 per cent, usually on some 40 something per cent of the vote. In contrast, coalition, multi-party governments, building blocks of a consensus democracy, are the norm in parliamentary systems where PR encourages multi-party systems and coalition governments.

SMPS facilitates single party government and encourages a *two party* system. The party system defines the number of parties that can realistically expect to win sufficient Commons seats to form a majority government. Save an extraordinary period of National Government in 1931–35 and the Wartime Coalition under Churchill in 1940–45, Labour and the Conservatives have alternated in office since 1922. The Liberal Party, and its contemporary successor, the Liberal Democrats, have not been in office by themselves since 1915. By performing better at the polls and having their vote concentrated in more constituencies, the two major parties, Labour and the Conservatives, win more seats. Other parties find their vote squeezed by these two hundred-pound electoral gorillas. If parties win votes but fail to win enough votes to win a particular seat, these votes are 'wasted' because they are not translated into seats. Under SMPS the only way the third party, the Liberal Democrats, can have a realistic expectation of being in government is either to win sufficient support to supplant the Conservatives as the second party, or have sufficient MPs to form a coalition government with Labour or the Conservatives in a hung parliament. The impact of SMPS is therefore to return a disproportional parliament, one in which the parties best placed to win individual seats will benefit, irrespective of their national performance. This encourages some degree of tactical voting, wherein electors vote against a party by voting for the party best placed to defeat it, abandoning their first choice party in the process. Because electors are persuaded that the third party, the Liberal Democrats, cannot form a government, they usually turn their attention to Labour and the Conservatives, often voting to help keep one or other out of government by defeating their candidate in a particular constituency.

That said, despite their under-representation, the Liberal Democrats increased their percentage of parliamentary seats from less than 2 per cent in 1979 to almost 8 per cent in 2001. While SMPS denies them the opportunity to form a single party government, it has not prevented the party from establishing the largest third party cohort of MPs since 1922. Without qualifying the impacts SMPS has on single party government, it is more correct to suggest it produces a 'two party plus' party system, rather than a simple two party system. Where the 1945–70 period was the classic era of two party majoritarianism (Butler and Stokes, 1974), the 1970–2001 period is best described as two party plus majoritarianism, as other parties, most notably the Liberals and nationalist parties in Scotland and Wales, grew in strength.

The post-1997 period has seen the further fragmentation of this two party plus system, although the emergence of a multi-party system at Westminster (and in government in Whitehall) remains stymied by SMPS. In Scotland and Wales, where the Scottish Parliament and the National Assembly for Wales are elected under a broadly proportional electoral system, the additional member system (AMS), we see a system of emergent multi-party politics. Under AMS, although both nations have been long dominated by the Labour Party in Westminster elections, Labour has to govern the devolved assemblies only in alliance with the third party, the Liberal Democrats. The electoral system denies Labour the majorities it would win under SMPS. As a result, the Scottish and Welsh party systems are in the process of diverging from the English party system, but it remains to be seen if this will have an impact on the UK party system as a whole.

Recent developments in Scotland and Wales, comprising only some 15 per cent of the UK's population, should not be overemphasized. The continued use of SMPS in elections to the House of Commons still determines the composition of the Westminster parliament. Westminster is still the site of government for 85 per cent of the UK population and it alone still wholly decides the budgets of the Scottish Parliament and the National Assembly for Wales (although Scotland may raise revenue at the margin if it chooses). Westminster alone determines all constitutional issues, macroeconomic, monetary, foreign and defence policy and European matters (see Chapter 2).

Over the past 30 years, then, the UK party system has changed, but in many ways it remains the same. The two party system dominated by Labour and the Conservatives has been significantly eroded, particularly in light of the post-1974 resurgence of the 'third party', the Liberal Democrats, and the growth in support for nationalist parties in Scotland and Wales. It has not, however, been overturned. So far the electoral system has ensured that one party holds all executive power by virtue of commanding a majority within a weak, reactive House of Commons.

As a result, the UK executive faces less checks and balances than do multi-party, coalitional counterparts in other countries. This is another structural feature of the UK majoritarian politics, part of the 'club ethos' of Westminster politics, and something that grants power to a strong, authoritative single party government. Unsurprisingly, the majoritarian model of democracy concentrates power in the hands of a majority, empowering fewer political institutions, while the consensus model does not, instead sharing and dispersing power among a greater number of political institutions. The UK prioritizes strong government rather than effective representation. Its electoral system continues to advantage fewer parties rather than more and it facilitates two party plus party politics and single party governments. In so doing it provides for a majoritarian form of politics.

SUMMARY

- Political parties are a key element in securing parliamentary democracy, but are not the only element.
- Institutional rules on voting greatly influence political outcomes.
- The single member plurality system (SMPS), sometimes called first past the post, strongly contributes to creating a single party government dominance in the UK.
- The traditional two party system is fragmenting, however.

9 CONCLUSION: THE UK AS AN EXEMPLAR OF A MAJORITARIAN DEMOCRACY

The analysis of political processes cannot be confined to a study of formal constitutions and of political institutions, however important these are. Politics involves state and non-state actors as well as institutions and citizens and organized political, social and economic interests. Yet, the interaction of these and other actors, resulting in the prioritization of certain issues, is facilitated by the structures of a particular liberal democracy. All actors owe their influence to the powers their particular office grants them. The power and authority of a prime minister comes from the office of prime minister, even if the holder's personal skills and resources enable him or her to make the most of what powers that office grants. Office confers certain actors with powers to do some things, but also restricts their ability to do others. Institutional settings affect both the policy reach and the policy grasp of all actors.

This is why understanding institutions and how they work is important. Different institutional structures, being particular to any political regime in a historically formed national setting, influence the practice of politics. They include the form of government, the constitution, the electoral system and the party system, all of which help determine how key institutions, among them the executive, the legislature and the judiciary, interact with one another and produce particular political outputs. The differences between majoritarian and consensus democracies and parliamentary and presidential regimes, a comparison between the UK and the USA, are illustrated in Table 1.8 (overleaf).

The UK executive is empowered as a single party government, thanks to the disproportionality of the single member plurality system and the two party plus system it encourages. It is therefore able, with parliamentary permission, to alter the constitution as it chooses and in ways electors tolerate.

We can therefore identify three key *structural* features of the UK political system:

- a flexible, easily amendable constitution
- a unitary state
- a parliamentary executive, able to lead a legislature elected under a single member plurality electoral system.

These provide for the two principal *powers* that are prime features of a UK's majoritarian political system:

- centralized government
- executive authority (provided, of course, as we have seen, that the executive has a reliable majority within the House of Commons).

TABLE 1.8 Systemic institutional differences between the USA and the UK

	USA	UK
System type	Presidential, federal.	Parliamentary, unitary.
Constitutional form	Fixed, inflexible. Altered only by super majority and with the joint agreement of centre and locality (two-thirds of the legislature and two-thirds of the 50 states having to be in favour).	Flexible. The constitution is easily altered by parliamentary legislation.
Centre–locality relations	Dispersed, power being shared among the federal government and the 50 states of the union. The constitution determines which authority exercises what powers.	Centralized, power being devolved from the centre.
Chief executive	President. Directly elected by popular vote.	Prime minister. Not directly elected, but drawn from the majority party in the House of Commons.
Executive form	Individualized. Led by the presidential chief executive.	Collective. Headed by the prime ministerial chief executive.
Legislative structure	Symmetrical bicameralism. Legislative power shared within the Congress between the Senate and the House of Representatives.	Asymmetrical bicameralism. Within parliament the elected House of Commons has considerably more legislative power than the unelected House of Lords.
Executive–legislative relations	Autonomous institutions based on the separation of powers. The agreement of both the president and the Congress is needed for legislation to pass.	Asymmetric, with the executive dominating the legislature, thanks to its majority in the House of Commons.
Judicial authority	Strong. A constitutional court, the Supreme Court, has the power to review and strike down policy decisions taken by the president and the Congress that are deemed to abridge rights set out in the constitution which government cannot challenge.	Weak. The judiciary is not able to review or strike down parliament's legislative decisions, because there is no higher constitutional standard by which parliament is judged.

The UK executive has to share a degree of power with other actors, but it is well resourced and therefore more authoritative than any alternative executive operating within a consensus democracy. Here, as Table 1.9 demonstrates, we can see that the UK is as good an exemplar of a majoritarian democracy as can be found.

TABLE 1.9 The Lijphart model applied to government in the UK

	Majoritarian elements	Consensus elements
Form of government	Unitary and centralized.	Decentralized forms of government established in Scotland and Wales, where devolved assemblies have been given powers over key elements of domestic policy, but covering only 15 per cent of the UK population.
Legislative structure	Concentration of legislative power in a unicameral legislature or in one chamber of a two chamber legislature.	
Constitutional form	Flexible constitutions that can be amended by simple parliamentary majority.	
Judicial review	The legislature has the final word on the constitutionality of their own legislation.	
Executive government	Concentration of executive power in single party government.	Coalition administrations in the Scottish Parliament and the National Assembly for Wales.
Executive–legislative relations	Executive–legislative relations in which the executive is dominant.	
Electoral system	House of Commons elected under single member plurality system, a majoritarian and disproportional electoral system.	Devolved assemblies in Scotland and Wales elected under the additional member system, which provides for a more proportional allocation of seats won from votes cast.
Party system	A two party system in terms of forming governments, the two party plus system in terms of representation in the House of Commons.	Multi-party systems in evidence within the Scottish Parliament and the National Assembly for Wales.

Devolution means that the UK now contains some elements of a consensus democracy, but it remains a majoritarian democracy. UK politics are still dominated by Westminster politics where the election of a single party government is facilitated by a plurality electoral system granting the largest electoral minority a parliamentary majority. The UK parliament can reform the flexible constitution at will, provided that the government is confident such actions will be rewarded and not punished by the electorate at a forthcoming election.

Our interest is in what the UK system 'is' rather than 'what it should be', so we can set aside normative judgements either praising or criticizing the UK's majoritarian system. Nor need we be concerned with whether centralization is a good or a bad thing. We can conclude, however, that consensus democracies divide and sub-divide power, both horizontally, within the federal government, and vertically, between central and local government. They therefore create more veto players able to block initiatives, something that often leads to gridlock and deadlock. In contrast, majoritarian governments, being centralist, can be more authoritative because they face far fewer veto players. They avoid gridlock but can suffer the pitfalls of producing ill thought-out policy initiatives, something often reflecting the pressures to deal with problems. Governmental hyperactivism, in which being seen to be doing something is as important as actually doing something, can sometimes be more of a problem than a solution; good or effective governance is not necessarily the preserve of authoritative government.

It should not be assumed that UK political institutions are all powerful, let alone omnipotent. Membership of the EU demonstrates this. Governments too often find, however well resourced they are, that politics is the 'art of the possible'. They discover they can do some things, but not others, even with a handsome parliamentary majority. The anticipated reaction of the electorate is a significant constraint hampering any government's freedom of manoeuvre, as are the criticisms of the news media and political opponents. The limits real life places on government are also considerable, from both within and outside the state. Governments are obliged to respond to a myriad of political realities, social crises and economic problems, and they are often as reactive as they are proactive. When asked what was the biggest obstacle to good government, Harold Macmillan, Prime Minister 1957–63, once famously replied, 'events, dear boy, events'. Political realities impose themselves upon the policy agendas of all political institutions, whatever form they may take.

Majoritarian and consensus democracies affect the conduct of politics in the most profound, significant ways. The very nature of UK politics is therefore bound up in the fact that a majoritarian model, one heavily influenced by tradition and hierarchy, provides for the centralization of power. In the UK, this is a quid pro quo for the powers of a stable and authoritative government, something provided for by the structures of an easily reworked constitution and its parliamentary system.

REFERENCES

Bagehot, W. (1963; first published 1867) *The English Constitution*, London, Fontana.

Bogdanor, V. (1995) *The Monarchy and the Constitution*, Oxford, Clarendon Press.

Bogdanor, V. (2003) 'Asymmetric devolution: toward a quasi-federal constitution?' in Dunleavy, P., Gamble, A., Heffernan, R. and Peele, G. (eds) *Developments in British Politics 7*, London, Palgrave Macmillan.

Butler, D. and Stokes, D. (1974) *Political Change in Britain*, London, Macmillan.

Dicey, A.V. (1959; first published 1885) *Introduction to the Study of the Law of the Constitution*, London, Macmillan.

Foley, M. (2000) *The British Presidency*, Manchester, Manchester University Press.

Gieben, B. and Lewis, P. (2005) 'Framing politics: the state in context' in Lewis, P. (ed.).

Hennessy, P. (2000) *The Prime Minister: The Office and its Holders Since 1945*, London, Penguin.

Lawson, N. (1994) 'Cabinet government in the Thatcher years', *Contemporary Record*, vol.8, no.3.

Lewis, P. (ed.) (2005) *Exploring Political Worlds*, Edinburgh, Edinburgh University Press/The Open University.

Lijphart, A. (1984) *Democracies: Patterns of Majoritarian and Consensus Government in Twenty One Countries*, New Haven, Yale University Press.

Lijphart, A. (1999) *Patterns of Democracy: Government Forms and Performance in Thirty Six Countries*, New Haven, Yale University Press.

Norton, P. (1993) *Does Parliament Matter?*, London, Prentice Hall.

Prokhovnik, R. (ed.) (2005) *Making Policy, Shaping Lives*, Edinburgh, Edinburgh University Press/The Open University.

Smith, M.J. (2005) 'Taking part in politics' in Lewis, P. (ed.).

FURTHER READING

Dunleavy, P., Gamble, A., Heffernan, R. and Peele, G. (eds) (2003) *Developments in British Politics 7*, London, Palgrave Macmillan.

Hay, C. (ed.) (2002) *British Politics Today*, Cambridge, Polity Press.

Hennessy, P. (2000) *The Prime Minister: The Office and its Holders Since 1945*, London, Penguin.

Kingdom, J. (2003) *Government and Politics in Britain*, Cambridge, Polity Press.

Lijphart, A. (1999) *Patterns of Democracy: Government Forms and Performance in Thirty Six Countries*, New Haven, Yale University Press.

Centre–periphery relations: government beyond Westminster

Montserrat Guibernau

Contents

1	Introduction	42
2	The making of the UK	44
	2.1 England	44
	2.2 Scotland	44
	2.3 Wales	46
	2.4 Northern Ireland	47
3	Nation, state and nation-state	50
4	Defining centre and periphery: national identities and UK politics	53
5	Governance beyond Westminster: the politics of devolution	56
	5.1 Devolution in Scotland	57
	5.2 How devolution in Scotland differs from devolution in Wales	59
	5.3 Devolution in Northern Ireland: a particular case	60
	5.4 Devolution in outline	63
6	Elected regional assemblies in England	65
	6.1 London	65
	6.2 English regions	65
	6.3 What is the main requirement for regional government? Is it a shared identity?	67
7	When was Britain?	68
	7.1 History	68
	7.2 On Britishness	70
8	Governance beyond the UK: the EU	71
	References	73
	Further reading	74

1 INTRODUCTION

This chapter explores centre–periphery relations in the UK, examining the contrast between those spaces where power and resources tend to concentrate (the centre) as opposed to those other areas which somehow become or are considered marginal (the periphery). The relationship between centre and periphery in the UK may be approached from many different angles: it can be explored with regard to economic, cultural or social activity, or in terms of the distribution of natural resources, the location of production and wealth, the urban versus rural distinction, and even the location of prestigious universities. Here, looking at the politics of devolution and the relationships between the various nations that constitute the UK, I begin by examining the transformation of the UK from a *centralized unitary state* into a *decentralized unitary state*.

In Chapter 1 Richard Heffernan defines the UK as a unitary state, one in which political power ultimately resides in a central and sovereign UK parliament. A unitary state, embracing one large political unit, can be contrasted to a federal state, comprising several political units. Unlike in a unitary state, the units of a federal state are not mere local or regional authorities subordinate to a dominant central power. Such units that form a federation are states with state rights themselves (Burgess and Gagnon, 1993, p.5). As Elazar (1997, p.12) argues, 'the very essence of federation as a particular form of union is self-rule plus shared rule'. Among many others, the UK, Spain, Italy and France are unitary states, while Germany, Canada, the United States of America, Switzerland and India are federal states.

A further relevant distinction, which impacts on the study of centre–periphery relations in the UK, concerns the difference between centralized and decentralized unitary states. A *centralized unitary state*, which governs its peoples from a central sovereign parliament, excludes the possibility of devolving any substantial powers to its territorially based minority national or ethnic groups. In some cases, the state may appoint a special representative for the area, responsible for the distribution of state subsidies and the administration of the area or region, but such a representative is usually accountable to the central parliament, not to a regional government (Guibernau, 1999, p.35). In contrast, a *decentralized unitary state* does devolve some powers to regionally elected institutions while ultimately maintaining the sovereignty of its central parliament. The degree of devolution varies in each case. It ranges from very minor decentralization structures, as illustrated by the division of France into *départements*, through the considerable political autonomy enjoyed by the 17 autonomous communities created in Spain after 1978, to the post-1997 devolution model adopted by the UK which provides differential degrees of political autonomy to the Scottish Parliament, the National Assembly for Wales and the Northern Ireland Assembly.

Centre–periphery relations in the UK are best explored by reference to the origins of modern Britain and the different histories of the nations that make up the contemporary UK. The complexity in this relationship can be illustrated by three approaches. First, by considering the connection between England, Scotland, Wales, Northern Ireland and the various regions within them. Second, by examining the relationship between London and other UK cities. Third, by exploring the internal complexities that arise from social, ethnic and religious differences and interests in the UK. Such complexities can be found within both the centre and the periphery.

This chapter also considers the politics of devolution in Scotland, Wales and Northern Ireland and looks at the prospects for regional government in England. At a supra-state level, centre–periphery relations are altered by the UK's membership of the European Union as regionalism plays an increasing role within the EU.

SUMMARY

State models can be divided according to whether power and sovereignty are or are not shared and devolved in the following ways:

- *Unitary state.* All powers reside in a central sovereign parliament. Power is not shared.
- *Federal state.* Constituted by sovereign units. Power is divided between one central and several regional governments.
- *Centralized state.* Excludes any form of devolution to its minority national and ethnic groups.
- *Decentralized state.* Prepared to devolve some powers to regionally elected institutions while retaining sovereignty in its central parliament.

2   THE MAKING OF THE UK

2.1   England

England played a dominant role in the medieval history of Britain, and the history of the UK is undoubtedly the history of the political and cultural domination of the English nation over those of Scotland, Wales and Ireland. In the making of the UK, each component nation played a different role: the English and Scottish kingdoms, the incorporation of Wales into the English Crown, and the subjugation of Ireland. The making of the UK was complex and fraught with violent confrontations, particularly virulent in the case of Ireland.

England's leading role in the creation of Britain can partly be explained by its ability, in the latter part of the Anglo-Saxon period, to annex and control smaller kingdoms under the rule of a single monarch. England enjoyed a common legal and fiscal framework, as well as a single church organization (Llobera, 1994, p.23). The Viking invasions did not radically change this picture nor erode the sense of English identity that had already been created. It is widely accepted that England was 'one of the first European countries to exhibit a sense of unity and identity, and that this was achieved long before the [Norman] Conquest. By the ninth century Alfred could be referred to as king of the English' (Reynolds, 1984; Greenfeld, 1992). It is remarkable that the Norman invasion of England in 1066, and the subsequent elimination of the indigenous aristocracy, did not bring about the centrifugal effects typical of feudalism in other Western European countries. Yet as William I superimposed an alien dynasty and aristocracy on an already structured and unified kingdom, the consequence of such a move was that provincial dynasties able to challenge the central power of the monarchy were eliminated in post-Norman England.

2.2   Scotland

Having enjoyed political independence until 1707, the survival of many of Scotland's institutions – notably its systems of law, religion and education – after Union with England contributed to the preservation of its singular identity. The different way in which Scotland was incorporated into the UK, through a monarchical take-over rather than by conquest (as was the case in Wales and Ireland), may account for the lesser impact the development of the UK exerted on Scottish distinctiveness.

In 1296, Edward I forced the submission of John Balliol, King of Scotland, with ease. Subsequently, William Wallace led national resistance against the English, winning the Battle of Stirling Bridge (1297), losing at Falkirk (1298) and executed in London (1305).

In 1306, Robert Bruce (Robert I) rose in revolt and was crowned the King of Scots, defeating the English army of Edward II at Bannockburn (1314). In 1320, the Scots Nobles sent a letter to Pope John XXII to persuade him of the legitimacy of King Robert the Bruce. This was a patriotic address known as the Declaration of Arbroath, invariably quoted as the first nationalist statement in Western Europe. The Declaration referred to Robert the Bruce as 'King of Scots', not King of Scotland, portraying the image of a limited monarch of a people, not only an owner of the land. Successively, James VI, King of Scotland, became King James I of England in 1603, adopting the title of 'King of Great Britain, France and Ireland' in October 1604.

Following the Civil War and the beheading of Charles I, England was proclaimed a free Commonwealth ruled by the army under Oliver Cromwell's leadership. Although Scotland immediately proclaimed King Charles II as monarch, Cromwell invaded and defeated Scotland to offset this. Subsequently, following the Restoration of the English monarchy in 1660, the Act of Union of Parliaments was passed in 1707 enacting a full and incorporating union between England and Scotland. This meant that the Scots finally lost their political independence.

In 1715, and again in 1745, the Jacobites attempted to break the Union, but were unsuccessful. Despite such opposition, it is open to debate whether the Scots consented to the Act of Union, or had it imposed upon them. Nonetheless, while Scotland was now governed at Westminster, the Union between England, Scotland and Wales did preserve the Kirk (the Scottish Church), as well as maintain distinctively Scottish forms of law and education, all of which contributed to a Scottish identity.

FIGURE 2.1   Presentation of the Treaty of the Union between England and Scotland to Queen Anne

2.3 Wales

In 1282, Edward I conquered Wales and the Statute of Rhuddlan (or Statute of Wales, 1284) established English rule. Rather than involve the assimilation of the Welsh by the English the conquest saw 'a colonial system ... established in those parts of Llywelyn's Principality which were by 1284 in the hands of the king' (Davies, 1991, p.166). In 1400, Owain Glyndwr led the most outstanding and successful rising in Wales against the new order and the tyranny of the English border barons, which almost led to the re-establishment of Welsh rule. Glyndwr sought to create an independent Wales that would have its own independent church and educational structure through the establishment of a system of Welsh universities. However, the accession of the Welsh Tudor dynasty to the English throne, following Henry Tudor's victory at the Battle of Bosworth Field in 1485, encouraged Welsh assimilation on the basis of equality with England. Wales was territorially structured according to the English model of the shires. Leading Welsh families held their land from the king, others became lease-holders and tenants after the English pattern, and the feudal aristocracy was received at the English court. But a deep breach, fostered by economic inequality, opened between landlord and tenant, one which remained unhealed for centuries.

FIGURE 2.2   Illustration of Owain Glyndwr

The Act of Union of 1536 was in response to Henry VIII's wish to incorporate Wales within his realm. It meant the complete administrative assimilation of Wales into the English system. Welsh customary law was abolished and English was established as the sole language of legal proceedings. In 1543 the Court of Great Session was constituted, a system of courts modelled on the practice already used in the three counties which, since 1284, had formed the municipality of North Wales. The Court of Great Session remained the system of higher courts of Wales until 1830, when, against considerable opposition, it was abolished.

The Catholic tradition died slowly in Wales under Elizabeth I and James I; Puritanism was strongly resisted and Oliver Cromwell had to employ oppressive measures to impose it. In the eighteenth century, Wales turned rapidly from the established church to embrace dissent with strong Calvinist leanings. In 1735, the church gathered large numbers of followers from the Church of England. This also helped contribute to the rise of an incipient Welsh nationalism, particularly as the desire to protect Welsh native culture from progressive Anglicization rose in the eighteenth century.

The Industrial Revolution transformed Wales, threatening the traditional ways of rural life, leading to protests such as the Rebecca Riots in 1843. Industrialization also prompted the radical exploitation of the mineral wealth of Wales, particularly coal, which additionally transformed the life of Welsh people. Chronic poverty and increasing unemployment intensified in Wales before and after the First World War, continuing almost unchecked until the Second World War as the Great Depression hit hard. After 1945, as the Labour government drew substantial support from its electoral socialist stronghold of South Wales, nationalization prompted a full-scale programme of industrial development. Yet, while the Scottish Office had been established in 1885, the Welsh Office was only set up in 1964. Here, while the Welsh celebrated their national identity, particularly in cultural terms, the political integration of Wales within the English-dominated UK meant than 'Welshness' was not as distinctive a national force as was 'Scottishness' north of the border.

2.4 Northern Ireland

Ireland was long considered a de facto province of England, a colonial possession dominated politically and militarily by its more powerful neighbour to the east. The English divided Ireland into counties for administrative purposes, introduced English law and established a Parliament in England and Ireland in 1297, within which only the Anglo-Irish were represented. By the fourteenth century Irish discrimination by the English had prompted widespread protests, which had resulted in a revival of the Irish language, law and culture, particularly as English power was seen to diminish. Yet, the recognition of Henry VIII as King of Ireland in 1541 led to the confiscation of monastic property and the isolation of would be rebels, many of whom had their lands confiscated. The beginnings of the Plantation of Ulster, the pronounced migration of Scots to the northern counties of Ireland, Ulster, dates from the beginning of the seventeenth century. Thus Ulster became a province dominated by Protestant, Scottish planters, while the native Irish, continuing to claim allegiance to the proscribed Catholic Church, became landless and displaced by the colonizers. The Plantation of Ulster can be considered as the starting point of an historical process which has resulted in the contemporary 'troubles' between Unionist and Republican, Protestant and Catholic.

In 1653 a union of the three kingdoms of England, Scotland and Ireland was secured. By this Act of Settlement, Ireland was portrayed as a conquered territory. By that time Ulster had become the most British and most Protestant part of Ireland, although a large Irish Catholic population was also located there, and the rest of Ireland remained Catholic. James II, a Catholic King of England, sought to reverse Roman Catholic discrimination, but was challenged by William III, a Protestant, who defeated him and his Catholic supporters at the Battle of the Boyne in 1690, an event still commemorated by Unionists in contemporary Ulster.

FIGURE 2.3 Contemporary wall mural of the Battle of the Boyne in Northern Ireland

At the beginning of the eighteenth century, the Williamite wars reinforced Catholic discrimination by imposing the Penal Laws excluding Catholics from the army, preventing them from taking part in politics and depriving them of access to education (Jenkins, 1997, p.93). Particularly repressive conditions in County Armagh gave rise to bitter sectarian strife. In 1795 a battle between Catholics and Protestants at the Diamond encouraged the creation of the Unionist Orange Society, which was later known as the Orange Order, organized to protect Protestant interests. The Act of Union of 1801 put Protestants under the formal protection of the British – now the Union – Parliament.

In 1829 Roman Catholics were emancipated, the British Test Act provided political equality for most purposes, but did little to alleviate discrimination in Ireland for all but the landed gentry. Still, the dramatic success of the Roman Catholic Daniel O'Connell's emancipation movement provoked Protestant hostility and led to its violent suppression in 1843. The nineteenth century witnessed a succession of Irish crises. Foremost among these was the Great Famine of the 1840s which desolated the countryside (Hayden, 1997), forcing large numbers of Irish people to migrate to the British mainland, North America, Australia and New Zealand. In Ulster, particularly in the industrial powerhouse of Belfast, Protestants held the monopoly of skilled jobs.

Catholics were to be mostly found in non-skilled jobs, a divide which still exists in contemporary Northern Ireland.

The late nineteenth century saw 'Britain's Irish Question' elevated to the top of the political agenda. Prompted by a conservative Irish nationalist movement, successive Liberal governments attempted to introduce some degree of Irish self-government in the form of 'Irish Home Rule'. Unsuccessful in 1886 and 1893, thanks to the determined opposition of Protestant Unionists and English Conservatives (and Liberal Unionists, too) a bill was finally passed in 1914, only for Home Rule to be postponed once the First World War began that August. Soon, however, the peaceful and conservative Irish campaign for Home Rule found itself displaced by a radical Republican movement for Irish independence, which organized an abortive uprising in Dublin at Easter 1916 which declared an Irish Republic. The harsh British repression of the Easter Rising, which saw the summary execution of the ringleaders of the revolt, lead to the rise of Sinn Fein, the emergence of a guerrilla force, the Irish Republican Army (the IRA), and the Irish War of Independence, 1919–21. Escalating violence further divided the country into the Republican majority and the Protestant minority located in the enclave of Ulster. It led to an unsustainable situation culminating in the Government of Ireland Act 1920 which divided the country into two self-governing parts.

As a result, Northern Ireland was formed by six of the nine counties of Ulster which remained within the British state. Ulster Protestants opposed leaving the UK and rejected the possibility of becoming a minority within a largely Catholic Irish state. The three remaining counties of Ulster, together with the 26 counties of the rest of Ireland, left the UK to become a dominion of the British Empire known as the Irish Free State. Eamon de Valera became its first president. In 1937, de Valera replaced the title of the Irish Free State with the word Éire (Ireland) and in 1949 Britain recognized Ireland as an independent republic and consolidated the position of Northern Ireland as a united province with England. Sadly, the partition of Ireland did little to promote a political settlement between the Unionist majority and the Republican minority in Northern Ireland. This inevitably lead to widespread conflict and a de facto civil war in the 1970s and 1980s, widening a political chasm which the post-1994 peace process and the paramilitary ceasefires have only begun to bridge.

SUMMARY

- England, Scotland and Wales are nations.
- Wales was conquered by the English in 1282 and its parliamentary union with England took palace in 1536.
- The *United Kingdom of Great Britain* was formed by the Act of Union of 1707, although the term Great Britain had been in use since 1603, when James VI of Scotland became James I of England (including Wales). Later unions created the United Kingdom of Great Britain and Ireland and, after 1921, the United Kingdom of Great Britain and Northern Ireland.

3 NATION, STATE AND NATION-STATE

Why do England, Scotland and Wales take part in the Six Nations rugby championship alongside Italy, Ireland and France? Are they all 'nations'? What do we mean by calling them 'nations'? The nation has become one of the most contested concepts of our times. Scholars, politicians and political activists present different definitions of the nation, usually focusing on a variety of cultural, political, psychological, territorial, ethnic and sociological principles. The lack of an agreement on what constitutes the nation suggests there is some difficulty in dealing with such a complex phenomenon. The crux of the matter probably embraces the link that has been established between *nation* and *state* and to the common practice of using the nation as a source of political legitimacy. Recognition as a nation grants different rights to a community that claims to comprise a single national unit. It usually implies an attachment to a particular territory, a shared culture and history and the assertion of the right to self-determination. Of course, as we shall see, nations are not internally homogeneous and are affected by internal and external migration flows. Yet, to define a specific community as a nation involves the more or less explicit acceptance of the legitimacy of the state which claims to represent that nation. If the nation does not possess a state of its own, it then implicitly acknowledges the nation's right to self-government involving some degree of political autonomy. This, in turn, may or may not lead to a claim for independence or secession from the state which claims sovereignty over the nation.

The nation, however, cannot be viewed in isolation and a clear-cut distinction has to be drawn between three main concepts: state, nation and nation-state. Max Weber defines the '*state*' as 'a human community that (successfully) claims the *monopoly of the legitimate use of physical force* within a given territory' (Weber *et al.*, 1991, p.78). The concept '*nation*' refers to 'a human group conscious of forming a community, sharing a common culture, attached to a clearly demarcated territory, having a common past and a common project for the future and claiming the right to rule itself' (Guibernau, 1996, p.47). This definition attributes five dimensions to the nation:

- psychological (consciousness of forming a group)
- cultural
- territorial
- political
- historical.

People who share such characteristics are referred to as having a common national identity. It is the sharing of a common national identity, expressed in terms of culture, language, religion, ways of life, common memories, shared past experiences and territory, that makes people feel they belong to the same community and have a certain degree of solidarity towards their fellow-nationals. However, a nation-state, being different from a nation and a state, has to be distinguished from the other two. The nation-state is a modern political institution. First, it is a state that both claims and exercises the monopoly of the legitimate use of force within a demarcated territory. Second, it is a state that seeks to unite the people subjected to its rule by means of homogenization, creating a common culture, symbols, values, reviving traditions and myths of origin, and sometimes inventing them. In seeking to engender a sense of belonging among its citizens the nation-state demands their loyalty and fosters their national identity.

The nation-state aspires to consolidate the nation where it already exists, but, should the nation-state rule over a territory containing different nations, parts of nations or ethnic groups, it tends to prioritize the culture and language of a particular nation. These then become dominant under the state's protection. For instance, at its inception, the Spanish state imposed the Castilian language and culture on the various peoples living within its territory, notably Catalonia and the Basque country, which had previously enjoyed their own independent institutions and laws. In the case of Catalonia, these institutions were dismantled after 1714 as Spanish troops conquered and occupied Barcelona.

The nation-state has exercised control of institutions and laws, the national media and the national education system. It has variously sought to nominate and promote a single official language, sometimes a single religion, and disseminated a specific version of the nation-state's history based on remembering, ignoring or forgetting certain key events, and recovering and inventing national symbols, ceremonies, rituals, heroes, sacred places and traditions. Such strategies have been consistently employed in order to create and sustain a homogeneous national identity among its citizens. However, numerous examples prove that very few nation-states have managed to successfully homogenize their populations. Differences have prevailed in spite of the nation-state's historical strategies to instil a common identity among its otherwise diverse citizenry.

The advancement of democracy in contemporary Western nation-states and the intensification of globalization processes have encouraged the re-emergence of nationalist movements representing oppressed or silenced nations that demand the right to self-determination. In the case of ethnic groups formed by people of immigrant origin, democracy has provided them with the tools to pursue the right to develop and practice their indigenous culture and language alongside those of the host country. One very important point in any theory of ethnicity concerns its dual nature: there is an ethnicity that members of a group claim and feel for themselves, but there is also the ethnicity which is attributed to them by others. There is also the more complex possibility that the claimed or felt ethnicity of group members may be shaped by that which is attributed to them by others. Although nation-states often corrode subordinate ethnicities, some nation-states may define themselves as 'multicultural' or 'multi-ethnic'. This is the case in the UK, and also in the USA and other countries.

The rise of sub-state forms of nationalism in Europe and elsewhere can be interpreted as being a product of globalization. The globalization of the economy and social relations has contributed to the transformation of the nation-state and also seems to have contributed to the intensification of regional forms of nationalism. Globalization, which involves greater awareness of diversity as it stresses interdependence between peoples, markets and cultures, is not an even process. Access to the technology that facilitates globalization is restricted to certain nations, individuals and groups being dependent on certain means and resources. On the one hand, globalization contains the potential for creating a world in which a greater number of cultures interact with one another. On the other, it also contains the potential for cultural homogenization, where a single culture expands globally to the detriment of other cultures. This perceived threat is one of the key factors contributing to the revitalization of minority cultures, many of which are struggling to find a niche in the global marketplace. Control over education and the mass media are crucial for nations who wish to promote their own languages and specific cultures. However, these nations should acknowledge that their languages and cultures will have to survive alongside more powerful ones that are gradually permeating – and influencing – all aspects of life. Minority cultures struggling to survive can only do so by entering an unequal contest with a major global culture.

One of the key elements in the construction of national identity is a shared history formed by memories of a community having suffered and thrived together. Making history not only involves selecting some specific events critical to the life of the nation, but also includes the collective forgetting of some events. It even leads to the modification and invention of memorable and dramatic experiences endured by the community. History emphasizes the transcendent character of the nation, expanding well beyond the life span of any individual. Equally importantly, history also portrays the nation as a community of fate.

SUMMARY

- The *state* is a political institution.
- The *nation* refers to a cultural community attached to a clearly demarcated territory, having a common past and a common project for the future and claiming the right to rule itself.
- The *nation-state* is a modern political institution, defined by a type of state which seeks to unite the people subjected to its rule by means of cultural homogenization.
- Most nation-states are not homogeneous and contain various minority national and ethnic groups within their territory.

4 DEFINING CENTRE AND PERIPHERY: NATIONAL IDENTITIES AND UK POLITICS

Why do British people speak 'English' and not 'British'? Why is it easier to travel from London to any British city than to travel from Bedford to Leamington Spa? Why are the National Gallery, the British Museum and Tate Modern all in London? Why does London house the Stock Exchange? This has to do with the pivotal role played by England in the constitution of the UK and by the designation of London as the capital of the UK.

Within any given country, we are likely to be able to establish a distinction between centre and periphery. The centre generally exerts political, economic and cultural power over the periphery, which is always dependent, tends to lack resources and often suffers from insufficient investment. The distinction between centre and periphery manifests itself, at least, at three different levels.

First, between the dominant nation or ethnic group within the country and the other nations and ethnic groups. For example, England's centrality in relation to Wales or Scotland. Second, between the country's capital city and other cities. For example, London in relation to Cardiff, Belfast or Edinburgh. Third, between different areas within the same nation. For example, the Scottish Lowlands, where the majority of the Scots live, the greatest concentration of Scottish industry is located and the main Scottish cities (Edinburgh and Glasgow) are placed, acts as a centre in relation to the Hebrides and the Highlands.

What are the consequences of being situated at the centre or in the periphery? If we return to the distinction between England and Scotland or Wales, we can observe that:

- England contains the capital city of the country in which the key institutions of the UK state are located.

- The Queen has her main residence in London.

- The greatest concentration of jobs and industry are in England, although it could be argued that England does not enjoy an even distribution of industry itself: in terms of prosperity the south-east predominates. This illustrates the notion that peripheries are also to be found within the centre and the other way round.

- All foreign consulates and embassies have their key representatives in London, although some of them may have further representatives in other cities.

- England was the heart of the British Empire and led the emergence of the Union by incorporating to itself, through various means, Wales, Northern Ireland and Scotland.

- English, the language which originated in England, has become the language spoken by the majority of the British people (although some British citizens may not be able to speak it, and the government has decided to implement some measures to change this and make competence in English a requirement for British citizenship). Also, English is the language spoken in a number of Commonwealth countries and those countries formed by a substantial number of immigrants originating in the UK; for example, the USA, Australia, New Zealand and Canada.

Therefore, we can see some of the consequences of being located at the centre. For instance, the centre holds the most powerful governance institutions, and it enjoys greater economic and financial activity, generally resulting in greater wealth. In short, the centre rules.

Now consider how the place where you live relates to others in terms of centre and periphery. You will discover that the same place may act as a 'centre' in some cases and as a 'periphery' in some other contexts. For example, Edinburgh represents the periphery when compared with London, but Edinburgh is the centre when considered in relation to Aberdeen or Lerwick. If we consider the EU, then Brussels stands as the centre and the UK and London are located in Europe's periphery, not only for geographical reasons but also because of the UK's decision not to join the euro. This illustrates the complexity of the centre–periphery relationship and the different factors that can be employed when measuring a city, a region, and even a country's status as a centre or periphery.

The struggle for power and resources, which takes place between the centre and the periphery but also takes place within the periphery, may complicate matters even further. For example, devolution to Northern Ireland has resulted in the enhancement of Belfast as a capital city, placed within the UK's periphery and turned into a stronger centre within Northern Ireland. Yet the existence of sharp internal divisions between Unionists and Republicans adds greater complexity to the development of Belfast and Northern Ireland in general. For instance, it could be argued that confrontation between radical sectors of the Unionist and the Republican communities reveal fragility and great difficulty in implementing any development project for the area. Hence, internal conflict within a periphery can result in the perpetuation of its peripheral status by hampering investment and disrupting development plans which, to succeed, require the support of the whole community. Yet, some Unionists feel that their dominant position within Northern Ireland is being threatened by devolution. For this reason, they fear and oppose change. In contrast, the majority of the Republican movement has supported devolution, although some have become disillusioned at the impasse the peace process has often found itself at, typified by the suspensions of the Northern Ireland Assembly and its power sharing executive. A long history of mistrust, suffering and violence cuts across both communities, factors which have undoubtedly played a key role in the perpetuation of Northern Ireland's peripheral status, marked by low investment, high unemployment and a lower standard of living than the rest of the UK.

A further question concerns how those who belong to the periphery feel about their own status. Usually, awareness of one's peripheral position is not very pleasant and people tend to develop a feeling of resentment against the privileges they perceive as being enjoyed by others. In the UK, the centrality of England has contributed to the fostering of nationalist feelings in both Scotland and Wales, which have been almost totally dependent on English rule exerted from London. The demand for some degree of autonomy for Scotland and Wales is closely connected with the desire of the Scots and Welsh to reverse the peripheral role their nations have played for centuries.

While nationalist movements in Scotland and Wales invoke various arguments, such movements invariably appeal to history, evoking the time when their nations were free and enjoyed their own independent institutions. They blame the homogenizing policies imposed by England for the weakening of their indigenous languages and cultures. Their grievances include complaints about lack of investment and English exploitation of their natural resources, as Scottish Nationalists claimed in regard to North Sea oil in the 1970s. A further argument employed by nationalists in Scotland and Wales, but also in Catalonia, Quebec, Flanders and Veneto, among many different nations without a state of their own, concerns their wish to strengthen democracy. In their view, devolution and self-determination, regardless of how they are defined, involve giving a voice to the people, increasing their participation and allowing those affected by decisions to have a greater influence over those decisions. This is why, among those who support nationalist claims in Scotland and Wales, we find not only people who invoke historical, cultural, symbolic and emotional arguments, but also those who see devolution as a further step in the development of democratic practices. This feeling was strongly felt among a substantial number of Labour activists and voters who were persuaded to embrace devolution even though they opposed the very idea of an independent Scotland.

After the 1997 general election the Labour government undertook a programme of far reaching constitutional reform that could well transform the UK from a unitary state, ruled by the centre, into a decentralized unitary state. Its programme of Scottish and Welsh devolution was a response to long-standing demands for autonomy advanced by some of the peoples of Scotland and Wales.

SUMMARY

- Within any given country, there is a distinction between centre and periphery.
- The centre exerts political, economic and cultural power over the periphery.
- The relationship between the centre and the periphery manifests itself in national and ethnic differences and at the city and the regional level.
- The distinction between the centre and the periphery finds expression in geographical, economic, political and cultural terms.
- The struggle for power and resources not only takes place between the centre and the periphery, but it also exists within the centre and within the periphery.

5 GOVERNANCE BEYOND WESTMINSTER: THE POLITICS OF DEVOLUTION

In its programme of devolution, the Labour government had to decide whether to adopt a *symmetric decentralization* model, which would confer an equal degree of devolution to the UK's constituent nations, or to implement an *asymmetric decentralization* model, which would grant differing degrees of autonomy to Scotland, Wales and Northern Ireland. They opted for the second model in an attempt to respond to different claims about self-determination and to react to different degrees of national identity emerging in Scotland and Wales.

The UK model stands in sharp contrast with the symmetric decentralization implemented in Germany after the Second World War, where all its *Länder* enjoy political autonomy, and in post-Francoist Spain, where its 17 autonomous communities are due to enjoy similar powers once the decentralization process is completed. Devolution in the UK has been confined to Wales, Scotland and Northern Ireland, omitting the 85 per cent of the population that lives in England, something which could be remedied if elected regional assemblies are created in England. Some argue that in this omission lies the inherent instability of the UK decentralization model, quite apart from the different devolution 'settlements' already in place for Wales, Scotland and Northern Ireland. In what follows, I examine the post-1997 UK devolution process. At this point, it is worth considering that democratic-, economic- and identity-based arguments are combined and play a different part in each of the following cases.

5.1 Devolution in Scotland

Scotland has endured a long and complicated process towards self-determination. In a 1979 referendum, the Scots voted in favour of the Labour government proposals to establish a Scottish Parliament, but, thanks to a special majority provision requiring at least 40 per cent of the registered electorate to vote in favour, devolution was rejected when only 32.9 per cent of the electorate voted in favour in the referendum.

Subsequently, after 1988, a Scottish Constitutional Convention comprising political parties (Labour and the Liberal Democrats, but not the Scottish National Party), churches, unions and other civic groups began campaigning for change. Once in government, Labour organized referendums on devolution, which were held on 11 September 1997; 74.3 per cent of the Scots who voted, voted for a Scottish Parliament and 63.5 per cent voted to give it tax-raising powers. Once the devolved institutions were established, Scotland's status within the UK was transformed. In domestic policy terms it is no longer governed by the Scottish Secretary of State based at Westminster, but by a Scottish Parliament elected by the Scottish people. The Westminster Parliament retains competence over foreign and defence policy, European matters and, crucially, macroeconomic policy. A First Minister heads the Scottish Executive, normally the leader of the party able to command the majority support of the Scottish Parliament.

FIGURE 2.4   Referendum campaigners for devolution in Scotland, 1997

The 1997 referendum result will not by itself entrench Scottish devolution (what the Westminster Parliament creates, it can still legally unmake), but it has certainly provided the Scottish Parliament with a moral and political legitimacy. Ultimately, the Scottish Parliament will secure its constitutional future by convincing the Scottish people of its relevance.

The absence of a UK written constitution able to respond to the above questions opens up a wide range of possibilities. The re-establishment of a devolved parliament in Edinburgh does not alter, in principle, the unitary character of the UK state since sovereignty continues to reside in Westminster. A Scottish National Party (SNP) majority in the Scottish Parliament could, of course, call for further autonomy and even for a referendum on Scottish independence.

The Scottish Parliament is composed of 129 members, 73 elected from single member constituencies and 56 additional members. Elections are held every four years. The first election to the Scottish Parliament took place in 1999, when turn-out was 58 per cent, but in the 2003 election, turn-out fell to 41.45 per cent. Table 2.1 shows the results for the 1999 and 2003 elections.

TABLE 2.1 Scottish Parliament election results: number of seats gained by different parties, 1999 and 2003

Political party	1999	2003
Labour Party	56	50
Scottish National Party	35	27
Conservative and Unionist Party	18	18
Liberal Democrats	17	17
Scottish Green Party	1	7
Scottish Socialist Party	1	6
Scottish Senior Citizens Party	0	1
Others	1	3

Source: The Electoral Commission, http://www.electoralcommission.gov.uk

The establishment of the Scottish Parliament provides an asymmetric picture of the UK. It is based on the recognition of Scotland as being different from the rest of the UK in terms of having a specific culture, tradition and way of life, all of which stem from its past as an independent territory. To some extent, then, devolution has weakened the image of Scotland as a periphery within the wider UK. It remains to be seen, however, if devolution has merely empowered an Edinburgh–Glasgow 'centre', leaving other, more remote areas of Scotland to be redefined as a new 'periphery'.

Scotland's place as a proud historic nation in the UK clearly acknowledges the multinational character of the UK state. Of course, post-devolution Scotland remains an integral part of the UK and the Queen continues to be the UK's Head of State, embracing Scotland and Wales as well as England. The Westminster Parliament is and will remain sovereign even though it has devolved law-making powers over a wide range of matters concerning Scotland to the Scottish Parliament. As a result, as we shall see, Westminster retains many key powers and responsibilities over Scotland.

5.2 How devolution in Scotland differs from devolution in Wales

Devolution for Wales, rejected by the Welsh in a 1979 referendum, was also part of the constitutional reform package of the Labour government. However, in September 1997, the Welsh voted for the establishment of a National Assembly for Wales. The referendum result in favour was far narrower than in Scotland. On a 50.3 per cent turn-out in Wales, only 50.6 per cent voted in favour, indicating a far less entrenched sense of political identity and difference from the rest of the UK on the part of the Welsh, particularly when compared with feelings in Scotland. Table 2.2 shows details of percentage turn-out at referendums and assembly elections in the UK.

TABLE 2.2 Turn-out at referendums and first and second elections for devolved assemblies in Scotland, Wales, and Northern Ireland, %

	Scotland	Wales	Northern Ireland
Referendum year	1997	1997	1998
Referendum turn-out	60.4	50.3	81.1
Voting for devolution	74.3	50.6	71.1
Voting for tax-raising powers (Scotland only)	63.5		
Year of first elections	1999	1999	1998
Turn-out in first elections	58	46	68.84
Year of second elections	2003	2003	2003
Turn-out in second elections	41.45	38	64.8

Source: The Electoral Commission, http://www.electoralcommission.gov.uk

The very choice of name, the National Assembly for Wales, indicates a difference from the Scottish Parliament. The Assembly is comprised of 60 members, 40 from single member constituencies and 20 additional members. It too is elected every four years. In contrast with the Scottish Parliament, however, the Assembly has no-tax raising powers. The Scottish Parliament is entitled to vary the rate of personal taxation by plus or minus three per cent, although the present Labour–Liberal Democrat majority has pledged not to use these powers for the lifetime of the parliaments elected in 1999 and 2003. Obviously, legislatures with tax-gathering powers are more powerful than legislatures without such powers. In addition, while the Scottish Parliament has primary legislative powers and full executive powers, the National Assembly for Wales has only secondary legislative powers. The Westminster government merely consults the Assembly and its Executive on proposed primary legislation each year. Executive functions previously enacted by the Secretary of State for Wales have been transferred to the Assembly. Table 2.3 shows the results of the elections of 1999 and 2003.

TABLE 2.3 National Assembly for Wales election results: number of seats gained by different parties, 1999 and 2003

Political party	1999	2003
Labour Party	29	30
Plaid Cymru	16	12
Conservative and Unionist Party	9	11
Liberal Democrats	6	6
John Marek Independent Party	0	1

Source: The Electoral Commission, http://www.electoralcommission.gov.uk

5.3 Devolution in Northern Ireland: a particular case

Devolution in Northern Ireland has been an integral part of the post-1994 peace process, which aims to share power between the two divergent communities, the Unionist-Protestant majority and the Republican-Catholic minority. All-party talks, chaired by the former US Senator George Mitchell, followed the 1997 renewal of the IRA ceasefire. The decommissioning of arms by the IRA was made into a condition to be met during the talks, but no specific date for its accomplishment was ever given. This position underlined the government's stance on the illegitimacy of the use of violence for political ends, but also stressed peaceful means to attain political aims previously pursued through the use of violence.

The British Prime Minister, Tony Blair, the Irish Prime Minister, Bertie Ahern, the then Secretary of State for Northern Ireland, Mo Mowlam, and the then US President, Bill Clinton, all put pressure on all sides to pursue the talks. Finally, the Belfast Agreement, also known as the Good Friday Agreement, was signed on 10 April 1998. The agreement, marking a major breakthrough in conflict resolution strategy, seeks to reconcile the Unionist desire that Northern Ireland remains a province of the UK with the Republican claim for an independent united Ireland free from English domination. The two contradictory objectives, which have provoked years of intense violence and suffering for the people of Northern Ireland, were to be resolved in an internal power sharing accord in which Unionists and Republicans would be represented, and an external agreement in which the UK and Ireland guarantee the national aspirations of both communities.

The principle on which the agreement was based was 'the achievement of reconciliation, tolerance, and mutual trust, and to the protection and vindication of the human rights of all' (*The Belfast Agreement*, 1998, p.1). It enshrined 'the total and absolute commitment to exclusively democratic and peaceful means of resolving differences on political issues' (ibid., 1998, p.1) and the endorsement of consent as a principle on the basis of which the people of Northern Ireland should decide on their future. All participants 'recognize the legitimacy of whatever choice is freely exercised by a majority of the people of Northern Ireland with regard to its status, whether they prefer to continue to support the Union with Great Britain or a sovereign united Ireland' (ibid., 1998, p.2).

The agreement provides for a democratically elected Northern Ireland Assembly with an inclusive, fully representative membership. Once fully established, the Assembly will exercise executive and legislative authority shared across both communities and safeguards will protect the rights and interests of all. The agreement also established a North–South Ministerial Council to develop consultation, cooperation and action between Northern Ireland and the Irish government on matters of mutual interest. A British–Irish Council, comprising representatives of the UK and Irish governments, devolved institutions in Northern Ireland, Scotland and Wales and, if appropriate, elsewhere in the UK, together with representatives of the Isle of Man and the Channel Islands, was also created with the aim of fostering harmonious, mutually beneficial relationships among the peoples of the British Isles.

Among the most controversial and delicate matters dealt with by the agreement were the provisions for the release of prisoners whose organizations maintain a 'complete and unequivocal ceasefire', and 'the decommissioning of all paramilitary arms ... in the context of the implementation of the overall settlement' (*The Belfast Agreement*, 1998, p.20). At the same time the agreement made provisions for changes in British security arrangements, reducing the numbers and changing the role of the armed forces deployed in Northern Ireland, removing security installations and ending emergency powers.

The agreement was endorsed by referendums in May 1998 when 71.1 per cent in Northern Ireland (turn-out 81.1 per cent) and 94.4 per cent in Ireland (turn-out 56.3 per cent) provided strong support for the peace process. Elections for the Northern Ireland Assembly were held in June 1998 and again in November 2003. The Northern Ireland Assembly (Stormont) is formed by 108 members elected by single transferable vote and six members from each of 18 Westminster constituencies. Because of the specific nature of Northern Ireland politics, the Assembly is based on a system of weighted majorities to ensure cross-community consent between Unionist and Republicans on all major issues. The First Minister, the Deputy First Minister and the executive are elected by a system that ensures the distribution of ministerial portfolios between all major parties. The executive committee is not bound by collective responsibility, and the committees and their chairs are appointed in proportion to party strengths, to scrutinize and advise on the work of each Executive Minister (Hazell, 2000, p.4). Table 2.4 shows the Northern Ireland Assembly election results for 1998 and 2003.

TABLE 2.4 Northern Ireland Assembly election results: number of seats gained by different parties, 1998 and 2003

Political party	1998	2003
Ulster Unionist Party	28	27
Democratic Unionist Party	20	30
Sinn Fein	18	24
SDLP	24	18
Alliance	6	6
UK Unionist Party	5	1
Progressive Unionist Party	2	1
Independent	1	1

Source: The Electoral Commission, http://www.electoralcommision.gov.uk

While more than half of Unionists – and the majority of Republicans – support the Belfast Agreement, implementing the peace process has been problematic, not least because it has provoked a profound split within the ranks of Unionism. Opponents of the agreement see it as a sell out, ushering in a united Ireland within which Protestants would lose their privileged status. In particular, Ian Paisley's Democratic Unionist Party (DUP) has grown in electoral strength within the Unionist community. In addition, Unionists and Republicans have consistently failed to reach agreement on establishing a lasting power-sharing executive. While paramilitary ceasefires have remained in place (although renegade Republicans formed the Real IRA, which killed 29 people in a horrific bombing in Omagh, the largest single loss of life in the modern history of Northern Ireland), disagreements over IRA decommissioning have led Unionists to refuse to share government with Sinn Fein, something that then required the UK government to suspend the executive and the Assembly. As a result, the UK has again had to govern the province from Westminster. At the time of writing, while ceasefires prevail, the peace process – and the agreement it sponsored – remains stalled, with both Unionists and Republicans still unable to reach a lasting, permanent agreement on establishing devolved government in Northern Ireland.

5.4 Devolution in outline

Through devolution, Westminster has devolved the following functions to the Scottish Parliament, the National Assembly for Wales and (once it is finally up and running) the Northern Ireland Assembly (Hazell, 2000, p.4).

- In all three administrations: health, education and training, local government (including finance), social services, housing, economic development, agriculture, forestry, fisheries, food, transport, tourism, the environment, sport, heritage, and the arts. The crucial difference between the Scottish Parliament and the National Assembly for Wales is that Scotland has unfettered control over these matters (subject to funding from Westminster), while Wales is obliged to implement and manage many decisions taken at Westminster, save in areas Westminster delegates to Cardiff.

- In Scotland only: the legal system, penal matters and policing (these matters may be transferred to Northern Ireland at a later date if the Secretary of State sees fit).

- In Wales only: the Welsh language.

- In Northern Ireland only: social security (but the legislation contains mechanisms to ensure parity of benefit rates), employment, and the civil service.

In financial terms all three administrations are funded by block grant from Westminster. This is up-rated annually by the 'Barnett formula', which adjusts allocations in line with comparable adjustments in England. Within the block grant there is complete spending discretion. In addition, the Scottish Parliament has power to increase or decrease the basic rate of income tax by up to three pence in the pound.

The following functions are reserved to the UK Parliament and government (Hazell, 2000, p.4):

- the constitution
- foreign affairs
- defence, national security, immigration
- macroeconomics, fiscal and monetary policy
- trade
- transport safety and regulation
- policing, penal matters, and the legal system (in Wales and Northern Ireland)
- employment legislation (in Scotland and Wales)
- the civil service (in Scotland and Wales).

One of the main post-devolution concerns, which still remains unresolved, involves the political role of MPs who represent Scotland and Wales at Westminster. A prominent Scottish opponent of devolution, the Labour MP Tam Dalyell, when representing the area once posed the so-called 'West Lothian question' asking why Scottish MPs should be allowed to vote on Westminster issues when Westminster MPs could not vote on West Lothian matters. For many this is a considerable problem, one that reflects the reality of asymmetrical political reforms.

New political institutions require some time to bed down. So far, however, devolution has not encouraged further demands for increased power for the devolved institutions, nor prompted talk of Scottish or Welsh secession from the UK. Contrary to the predictions of Conservative (and some Labour) critics the UK remains a unified country. Devolution has, however, triggered two major debates. First, about the nature of British identity. Second, about the issue of expanding devolution to make it a symmetrical process, including England, particularly London and the English regions.

SUMMARY

- In 1997, the newly elected Labour government set in motion the *asymmetric decentralization* of the UK by granting differing degrees of political autonomy to Scotland, Wales and Northern Ireland.

- In 1997 referendums on devolution where held in Scotland and Wales. Their affirmative outcome in favour of devolution cannot of itself deliver constitutional entrenchment, but might reinforce its moral and political legitimacy.

- The Belfast Agreement, signed 10 April 1998, represented a major breakthrough in conflict resolution strategies. It stood for 'the total and absolute commitment to exclusively democratic and peaceful means of resolving differences on political issues' (*The Belfast Agreement*, 1998, p.1) and endorsed *consent* as a principle on the basis of which the people of Northern Ireland should decide on their future.

6 ELECTED REGIONAL ASSEMBLIES IN ENGLAND

6.1 London

London's population and economic size are those of a region. As such it contains various peripheries within itself. Further to this, there are some issues, mainly economic planning and transport, which are closely connected with the rest of south-east England. The Labour government introduced a Greater London Authority (Referendum) Bill in October 1997 and organized a referendum on 7 May 1998 in which 72 per cent voted (on a low turn-out of 33.5 per cent) in favour of establishing a Mayor and Assembly for London. Established after elections in May 2000 the directly elected Mayor and elected Greater London Authority (GLA) has a 'strategic' rather than a service provider role, embracing transport, economic development, the environment, planning, police, fire and civil defence, and culture.

6.2 English regions

At present, regional government in England is divided between local government and central government agencies. Eight English regions have a tripartite structure with responsibilities and powers divided in each region between the Government Office for the region (GO), the Regional Development Agency (RDA) and the Regional Chamber (most of which have now renamed themselves Regional Assemblies).

The Labour government established Regional Development Agencies (RDAs) in April 1999. The role of the RDAs, appointed by Ministers in London, is limited with primarily strategic functions based around preparing an economic strategy for their region. They are totally dependent on central government for their modest budgets. In terms of their powers, functions and political authority they are much weaker than the Scottish Parliament and the Welsh and Northern Ireland assemblies.

Government Offices for the regions were initially created in 1994 as 'Integrated Regional Offices',

> bringing together the regional functions of the Departments of Transport, Environment, Employment, and Trade and Industry. Their boundaries were used for Regional Development Agencies for speed and convenience (with the

exception of Merseyside, absorbed into the North-West in 1996). The offices were initially conceived of as representatives of the centre in the regions. Policy programmes remained under the sponsorship of individual departments.

(Sandford and McQuail, 2001, p.30)

Whereas Regional Chambers are

voluntary bodies containing approximately 70 per cent elected local authority representatives and 30 per cent 'social and economic partners' (SEPs). All Chambers have now been 'designated' by the Secretary of State under the Regional Development Agencies Act 1998, obliging the relevant RDA to 'take account of' their comments on its Regional Economic Development Strategy. This is their sole statutory role.

(Sandford and McQuail, 2001, p.31)

The devolution process implemented in Scotland, Wales and Northern Ireland has prompted fresh demands for elected assemblies in some English regions. The creation of Constitutional Conventions, inspired by the Scottish Constitutional Convention, in six English regions seeks to foster a greater public debate on devolution. The first Constitutional Convention was set up in the north-east in 1998. The north-west and Yorkshire followed in 1999, and the West Midlands, the south-west and the Cornish Constitutional Convention in 2000. In 1999, the Campaign for the English Regions was launched as an umbrella group for the Constitutional Conventions.

David Marquand and John Tomaney (2000) cite four reasons in favour of directly elected regional government in England:

- a tier of regional government already exists, but it is fragmented and poorly coordinated
- too much public policy is designed centrally in ways that do not match local conditions
- there is insufficient democratic scrutiny of the state both at a national and a regional level
- English politics needs to accommodate greater diversity and pluralism if it is to survive and promote greater participation in elections.

Some of the objections against elected regional assemblies have been considered by Sandford and McQuail (2001). These include:

- *Equity*, in regard to maintaining common national standards in health care, education and certain other key services.
- *Risk of failure* in the face of the considerable government intervention in setting standards, and the lack of confidence in existing regional structures.
- *Turbulence*, depending on the range of functions proposed, the transfer of power could be a complicated and turbulent process with considerable transitional costs.
- *Scepticism* about whether there are substantive arguments for change.

- *Vested interests*, including inertia, concerning 'the way in which England's administration, famously centralized, hangs together as a whole, and the weakness of regional identity that is another aspect of inertia'. *Whitehall*, referring to institutional resistance to change, and *Ministers*, that points to 'the extent to which Ministerial rewards and motivation at present turn on their command over functions organized centrally and not territorially' (Sandford and McQuail, 2001, p.59).

6.3   What is the main requirement for regional government? Is it a shared identity?

If we compare the UK with other Western democracies such as Spain, Italy or Germany – all endowed with decentralized structures allowing various degrees of political autonomy for their regions – we discover that strong regional identity, as in Catalonia, the Veneto and Bavaria, is always a very important feature. However, some newly created regions such as La Rioja and Madrid in Spain also exercise devolved powers. What unites them is a common interest; the belief that regional government may generate economic prosperity and a shared awareness that devolution may improve services, deepen democracy and, in most cases, reduce their peripheral status.

For instance, the creation of Spanish political autonomous institutions has added to the dynamism of civil society, generating a sense of common regional identity where it did not previously exist, and strengthening it where it was little more than a weak idea. Devolution has contributed to the generation of regional identity by creating and promoting regional flags, anthems, folklore, cultural traditions and art. While some of these elements originate in the local cultures now integrated within the boundaries of the autonomous community, others are the product of invention. It is interesting to note that whether indigenous or invented, cultural distinctiveness both generates and strengthens the collective identities of each autonomous community. It is possible to conclude that devolution – and with it, the creation of regional institutions corresponding to autonomous communities lacking prior historical or cultural identities – is often conducive to the emergence and strengthening of separate regional identities. Nowhere more so for Spain's historical nations – Catalonia, the Basque country and Galicia – where there is a clear connection between past and present experiences of autonomous institutions, law and a separate political and cultural identity that accounts for the sheer force of nationalist feelings.

SUMMARY

- The Labour government introduced a Greater London Authority (Referendum) Bill in 1997. The referendum took place in 1998. A Mayor and Assembly for London were first elected in 2000.

- At present the eight English regions have a tripartite structure with responsibilities and powers divided in each region between the Government Office for the region (GO), the Regional Development Agency (RDA) and the Regional Chamber (most of which have now renamed themselves as Regional Assemblies).

- Devolution has resulted in the strengthening of regional identities where they previously existed but it has also contributed to the generation of 'new' regional identities where they did not previously exist.

7 WHEN WAS BRITAIN?

7.1 History

So far, I have provided a brief historical background for England, Scotland, Wales and Northern Ireland, one that accounts for their distinctive identities and for the origins of their differing role within the UK. I have also defined devolution as an asymmetric decentralization process which responds to the claims advanced by the nations constituting the UK state. What, then, do we mean by Britain? Is it a nation? If so, when did the British nation begin to exist? The historian Linda Colley locates the birth of the idea of Britain after 1707. She describes war, religion and the prospect of material advantages as the three main factors that called the British nation into being.

> War played a vital part in the intention of a British nation after 1707, but it could never have been so influential without other factors, and in particular without the impact of religion. It was their common investment in Protestantism that first allowed the English, the Welsh and the Scots to become fused together, and to remain so, despite their many cultural divergences. And it was Protestantism that helped to make Britain's successive wars against France after 1689 so significant in terms of national formation. A powerful and persistently threatening France became the haunting embodiment of that Catholic Other which Britons had been taught to fear since the Reformation in the sixteenth century. Confronting it encouraged them to bury their internal differences in the struggle for survival, victory and booty.

... the Protestant worldview which allowed so many Britons to see themselves as a distinct and chosen people persisted long after the Battle of Waterloo, and long after the passing of the Catholic Emancipation Act in 1829 as well. For most Victorians, the massive overseas empire which was the fruit of so much successful warfare represented final and conclusive proof of Great Britain's providential destiny. God had entrusted Britons with empire, they believed, so as to further the worldwide spread of the Gospel and as a testimony to their status as the Protestant Israel. And this complacency proved persistent. Well into the twentieth century, contact with and dominion over manifestly alien peoples nourished Britons' sense of superior difference.

... impressive numbers of Britons did make the step from a passive awareness of nation to an energetic participation on its behalf. But they did so in the main not just because patriotism was recommended from above, but also because they expected to profit from it in some way.

(Colley, 1992, pp.387, 388, 391)

According to Colley, the British nation is a recent invention, created in 1707, and superimposed on much older allegiances. In Britain, localism remained strong until the introduction of conscription in the First World War. This explains why, for more than 50 years after the Union, the relationship between Scotland and the rest of Britain was fraught with suspicion, as was the relationship between Lowland Scotland and the Highlands. But the lucrative gains to be obtained from the expanding British Empire, as well as the passage of years, contributed to smooth internal differences within the Union, though they never faded away completely. Yet, as Colley argues, 'by 1837, Scotland still retained many of the characteristics of a distinct nation, but it was contained within a bigger nation. It was British as well as Scottish. By contrast, Wales was rather more distinct. Possessed of its own unifying language, less urbanized than Scotland and England, and – crucially – less addicted to military and imperial endeavour, it could still strike observers from outside its boundaries as being resolutely peculiar to itself' (Colley, 1992, pp.393–4).

Scottish and Welsh distinctive cultures and languages initiated a progressive decline after the Union with England; such decline was only partially altered by the influence of the romantic ideas about the value of distinctive cultures and languages which spread throughout Europe during the second half of the nineteenth century. Romanticism contributed to the assertion of Scottish and Welsh identity and gave rise to embryonic nationalist movements that, in the first instance, defended cultural objectives which, in time, evolved into fully fledged nationalist movements demanding self-determination.

Ireland enjoyed quite a different relation with the British Empire due to it being treated by London as a colony. The Catholics outnumbered the Protestants and since the invention of Britishness was so closely bound up with Protestantism, with war with France and with the acquisition of empire, Ireland was rarely able or willing to identify with it.

7.2 On Britishness

Earlier in this chapter I considered how Scotland, Wales and Northern Ireland came to be included in the UK. That incorporation was often not free from conflict, resistance, war and military intervention. Hence, as well as cooperation and a common fellowship, suspicion, lack of trust, sometimes hatred, expressed in various forms, have characterized the relationship between England, the leading power, and those nations which were annexed or conquered by it or amalgamated with it.

Modern nationalism in Scotland and Wales has been fuelled by the desire for democracy to be strengthened, for citizens to have a voice and proper representation, and by the wish for greater prosperity, investment and economic development to reverse the peripheral role of these areas, compared with England (and with London in particular). Nationalism has also been fuelled by memories of oppression, a lack of recognition, and having insufficient power and resources to develop their nations and the elements that constitute their specific identities. This, among other issues, could account for the precarious survival of Gaelic and the low number of Welsh speakers. A situation that, when applied to the English regions, could also account for the practical disappearance of Cornish.

Most UK nations enjoyed some of the benefits the British Empire brought to the centre. The empire was so vast, diverse and rich it conferred an unprecedented world status on the British as a whole. In this instance, the formation of another periphery, the empire, helped for a time to smooth over differences between the earlier centre and its peripheries.

In the twenty-first century, however, Britishness seems a fragile concept. Many factors are affecting British identity, among them decolonization, the questioning of the monarchy, the setting up of devolved institutions in Scotland, Wales and Northern Ireland, and, perhaps most significantly, Britain's increasing ethnic diversity, prompted mainly by the settlement of large migrant communities originating from the former British Empire, in particular the Indian subcontinent and the Caribbean. A further ingredient might be the decline in the habit of equating British with English, an equation automatically excluding non-English people. Thus, at a time when the Scots and the Welsh are reasserting their separate identities, the English will have to reconstruct their own distinct identity. Being British requires a more inclusive definition of Britishness, one capable of embracing all the peoples of the UK regardless of regional and local allegiance. Being English, Scots, Welsh and Irish in Northern Ireland is just one way of being 'British'. Finally, UK membership of the EU and the prospect of further European integration, not least the possible adoption of the euro, has served to question an already increasingly uncertain British identity. So much so, passionate reactions against European integration has led some to portray the EU as a threat to UK sovereignty and its historic identity.

SUMMARY

- The historian Linda Colley locates the birth of 'Britain' after 1707. She mentions three main factors that contributed to establishing the British nation: war, religion and the prospect of material advantage.

- The creation of the UK was not free from conflict, resistance, war and military intervention.

- The British Empire generated a unique opportunity for most UK nations to participate and enjoy some of the benefits it brought. Their peripheral status was temporarily overwhelmed by a new periphery in the empire.

- In the twenty-first century, Britishness is being redefined and an English identity is struggling to emerge as a distinct category separate from British identity. The two had been considered synonymous.

8 GOVERNANCE BEYOND THE UK: THE EU

One of the elements invoked in favour of regional devolution involves the significance of regions within the European Union. While some refer to the principle of subsidiarity (governing, when possible, at the local level), as promoted by the EU, as an argument in favour of devolution, others emphasize that regional government improves the prospect of receiving EU regional subsidies. At the moment, there are striking differences between regions within Europe. While some regions have an economic, administrative or geographical basis, but a negligible or absent cultural heritage, others such as Scotland (UK), Catalonia (Spain), Flanders and Wallonia (Belgium) display a powerful cultural distinctiveness and are often referred to as 'nations without states' (Guibernau, 1999). The EU does not distinguish between the two.

Evidence of regional economic advantage began to emerge in the 1980s. The dynamics of the single market and the rising significance of European regional policy have encouraged the emergence of a new kind of innovative, specialized economic region oriented towards the global economy. The 1988 reform of the Structural Funds (resources designed to support national and regional convergence within the EU) and the new opportunities generated by the single market (designed to complete EU economic integration) contributed to a general move towards indigenous growth at the regional level (Cooke *et al.*, 1997). Poorer regions benefited from changes in the Structural Funds, while better-off regions took advantage of the new opportunities provided by the single market; for instance, the 'Four Motors of Europe' (a cross-frontier collaboration involving Baden-Württemberg, Rhône-Alps, Lombardy and

Catalonia, which has recently been joined by Wales) attracted European funds and foreign investment.

The Committee of the Regions was set up in 1994 under the Treaty on European Union (the Maastricht Treaty). The Committee of the Regions (CoR), which aims to represent the interests of regional and local authorities in the EU, is made up of 222 independent representatives of regional and local authorities. These representatives are nominated by EU member states and appointed to a four-year term by the European Council. The mixture of regional and local representatives within the CoR undermines its character as a regional body, which has sparked great controversy among its potential and actual members, especially since there are no rules about how the fixed number of representatives from each country is distributed between the various levels of regional and local authorities.

The EU's embrace of regionalism seeks to reverse, or at least mitigate, the peripheral role of regions. Within the EU – a quasi-supranational institution founded and governed by nation-states – regions, already peripheral within their own nation-states, may feel even more remote from the EU core. Relatively powerful regions that enjoy self-determination within their own nation-states lack direct representation in EU institutions. The European Convention, chaired by Valery Giscard d'Estaing, which drew up a proposed new EU Constitution in 2004, received numerous demands from regional bodies and movements throughout Europe seeking regional representation within EU institutions. For instance, the citizens of 75 EU regions already enjoying devolved legislative powers, some 56.3 per cent of the EU's total population, unsuccessfully demanded the recognition of their legislative and administrative relevance (European Convention, 2002).

Although the CoR has to be consulted by the Council of Ministers and the European Commission with regard to health, culture, promotion of general and vocational training, trans-European networks and structural and regional policy, it is merely an advisory body. Its opinions are not binding. As such, because of the CoR's limited scope and influence within the EU, the idea of a Europe of the Regions, which citizens of 'nations without states' desire, is far from being a reality, although the very existence of the CoR does represent the significance regional Europe may acquire in the future (Guibernau, 1999, pp.172–3).

The process towards an eventual regionalization of the European Union is still in its early stages. There are striking differences between various European regions and it is unlikely that all of them will obtain the same degree of political autonomy and recognition within the EU. It seems certain, however, that a new and unprecedented process, by which selected nations without states, such as Scotland, Wales, Catalonia and Flanders, achieve cultural, economic and political relevance, has already been initiated.

For some, the UK still plays a peripheral role within the EU. The core resides in the Franco-German axis. Historically, the UK has stood at the edge of Europe. Its propensity to not seek the initiative in promoting European integration is best illustrated by its refusal, to date, to enter the single currency. This further demonstrates the different centre–periphery roles that states, nations and cities may play according to different environments. Of course, the EU was itself formed from very different types of regions and nations, some of which had a well established clear, separate geographical, administrative or economic identity, while others had only a strong sense of cultural identity and a desire for greater political autonomy, but lacked the means to advance such interests and objectives. The European regional movement seeks to reverse, or at least ameliorate, the peripheral role many regions play within EU institutions, which are largely dominated by key nation-states.

REFERENCES

The Belfast Agreement (1998) London, The Stationery Office.

Burgess, M. and Gagnon, A.G. (1993) *Comparative Federalism and Federation*, London, Harvester Wheatsheaf.

Colley, L. (1992) *Britons: Forging the Nation 1707–1837*, London, Vintage.

Cooke, P., Christiansen, T. and Schienstock, G. (1997) 'Regional economic policy and a Europe of the regions' in Heywood, P., Jones, E., Rhodes, M. and Wright, V. (eds) *Developments in West European Politics*, London, Macmillan.

Davies, R. (1991) *The Age of Conquest, Wales 1063–1415*, Oxford, Oxford University Press.

Elazar, D. (1997) *Exploring Federalism*, Tuscaloosa, Alabama, University of Alabama Press.

The Electoral Commission, http://www.electoralcommission.gov.uk (accessed 8 February 2004).

European Convention (2002) paper presented by regions with legislative powers within the EU, CONV 321/02, Marienhamm (Aland Islands), Helsinki/Brussels, 4–7 October.

Greenfeld, L. (1992) *Nationalism: Five Roads to Modernity*, Cambridge, Mass., Harvard University Press.

Guibernau, M. (1996) *Nationalisms*, Cambridge, Polity Press.

Guibernau, M. (1999) *Nations without States: Political Communities in the Global Age*, Cambridge, Polity Press.

Hayden, T. (ed.) (1997) *Irish Hunger: Personal Reflections on the Legacy of the Famine*, Dublin, Wolfhound.

Hazell, R. (2000) *The State and the Nations*, London, The Constitution Unit, University College London.

Jenkins, R. (1997) *Rethinking Ethnicity*, London, Sage.

Llobera, J. (1994) *The God of Modernity*, London, Berg.

Marquand, D. and Tomaney, J. (2000) *Democratizing England*, London, The Constitution Unit, University College London.

Reynolds, S. (1984) *Kingdoms and Communities in Western Europe 900–1300*, Oxford, Clarendon Press.

Sandford, M. and McQuail, P. (2001) *Unexplored Territory: Elected Regional Assemblies in England*, London, The Constitution Unit, University College London.

Weber, M., and Gerth, H.H. and Wright Mills, C. (eds) (1991) *From Max Weber: Essays in Sociology*, London, Routledge.

FURTHER READING

Guibernau, M. (1999) *Nations without States: Political Communities in the Global Age*, Cambridge, Polity Press.

Hazell, R. (2000) *The State and the Nations*, London, The Constitution Unit, University College London.

Marquand, D. and Tomaney, J. (2000) *Democratizing England*, London, The Constitution Unit, University College London.

Citizens and politics: modes of participation and dissent

Mads Qvortrup

Participation & dissent

Contents

1	Introduction	76
2	The context of participation and dissent	76
3	Assessing political participation	80
4	Citizens as voters: party identification	85
5	Recent theories of electoral choice: class voting and its alternatives	91
	5.1 The traditional model	91
	5.2 The 'revisionist' alternative	93
	5.3 The 'economic voting' model as an example of issue voting	94
6	Framing public opinion: the mass media, political participation and spin	95
	6.1 Role of the mass media	95
	6.2 How public opinion is organized: the politics of spin doctors	97
7	Conclusion	101
	References	102
	Further reading	103

1 INTRODUCTION

Democracy – the rule of the people – means that although the day-to-day powers of legislation and implementation are exercised through elected representatives and governments, citizen power and the ability to influence political developments extend beyond merely voting in elections. **Smith (2005)** has discussed a range of issues regarding participation and dissent in a comparative perspective; here, my focus will be on the UK. In exploring the many ways in which individuals and groups influence political developments, we shall consider the following questions.

- What is the nature of political participation in the UK in electoral and other arenas?
- Is it rational to vote?
- Do women participate more than men?
- Why do people demonstrate or riot?
- What makes some citizens vote for protest parties?
- Does the press influence the way we vote?
- What is extra-parliamentary politics?

In this chapter we first turn our attention to how we define political participation.

2 THE CONTEXT OF PARTICIPATION AND DISSENT

We are citizens, but we are also subjects (Wright, 1994). We are ultimately the authors of our own laws, but we are also bound by the laws of the land. We have a right to participate, but we also have responsibilities for maintaining the system (for example, by paying taxes, by ensuring school attendance for our children, and by serving as jurors). It is commonplace to decry the crisis of democracy – the seemingly relentless drop in turnout rates in parliamentary elections is met with almost universal complaint, not least by the news media. This is not surprising, perhaps, particularly if gloomy news sells newspapers! As every journalist will tell you, there is little mileage in good news.

Are matters as dire as the doomsayers will have us believe? Not necessarily, as **Smith (2005)** has recounted. There are other forms of participation apart from voting in elections. Participation is a broad category that covers many other activities, among them signing a petition, becoming a grass-roots activist, being a member of the local PTA, going on strike, writing letters to the local newspaper, and hurling stones at the police in violent mass demonstrations. Voting is but one form of political participation.

Political participation has been defined as 'those legal acts by citizens that are more or less directly aimed at influencing the selection of government personnel and/or the actions they take' (Verba *et al.*, 1978, p.1). This definition seems too restrictive: while it covers voting, campaign activity (such as campaigning for a local parliamentary candidate) and communal activity (attending meetings in the community), it is questionable whether the word 'legal' is essential. Indeed, illegal mass protest (participation in banned demonstrations) is often politically significant. Who would claim that the mass protests against the Communist regimes in Eastern Europe in 1989 were apolitical? A definition of political participation must cover all actions aimed at influencing decision making and political elite selection in a society. It will, therefore, include dissent as a form of participation (see **Smith, 2005**).

Clearly, drawing up a list of activities tells us little about the political significance of political participation. Citizen politics must be put in their own context. Sometimes political participation is spontaneous, and sometimes it is not. Some forms of 'reformist' participation are aimed at changing society (anti-globalization protests), others are more 'conformist' and directed at maintaining the status quo (the Countryside Alliance's mass rallies in support of fox-hunting). It can also be publicly instigated, or initiated by citizen action. Whatever its form, citizen politics is based on the premise that citizens can and do play an effective and efficient role in the political process. This is a not unimportant fact, yet it is worth bearing in mind that, in the past, citizen involvement has only occurred in very exceptional circumstances.

Why do citizens become involved in politics? What motivates them? One cause favoured by political sociologists is that social class and educational background determine civic political activity. Others believe that political attitude or membership of organizations is responsible for engagement in citizen politics. Yet, political activity can also be a result of dissent, stemming from unhappiness at the actions of the state. Students of citizen politics need to understand *when* citizens participate in politics – but they also need to understand *why* citizens get involved. Analysts of participation seek to understand *what* determines, say, voting behaviour and various forms of social protest. Some believe that political institutions can increase electoral turnout (the propensity for citizens to vote); others suggest that cultural factors play a more important role; and still others believe that citizen politics is a result of social factors (a higher level of education may lead to more political participation).

Political sociologists have undertaken their quest for relevant facts concerning political participation using a variety of techniques, above all quantitative surveys. One of the most comprehensive is the World Values Survey (see **Lewis, 2005**), which asked people from most countries around the world about their attitudes to a wide variety of topics. Another ambitious survey is the Eurobarometer Survey, which is carried out among member states of the European Union (EU). Both surveys suggest that the British are fairly active participants in their societies, and from Table 3.1 you can see that their activities are roughly comparable to those of other large EU countries such as France and Germany.

TABLE 3.1 Citizens involved in political activities in France, Germany and the UK (percentages of active citizens engaged in various activities)

Activity	France (%)	Germany (%)	UK (%)
Signing a petition	51	55	75
Campaign activity	7	3	8
Mass protest (lawful demonstrations)	31	25	15
Unlawful protest	10	2	8

Source: adapted from Dalton, 1996, p.76 (original data from *World Values Survey*, 1990)

Some of these figures speak for themselves, but others require some analysis. The British are considerably more likely to sign petitions than are the Germans and the French (in the UK, 75% did so; while 51% did so in France and 55% in Germany). The British are fairly active in political campaigns, but rather unlikely to participate in mass protests. While less than 20% of UK respondents have been engaged in mass protests and demonstrations, almost 33% of French citizens have been engaged in such activity. There are undoubtedly cultural reasons for this pattern. French politics is shaped by the cultural mythology of mass protest. Protest is an integral part of the way that French activists see themselves; it is perhaps indicative that two of the most quoted works in political philosophy in France in the twentieth century were, respectively George Sorel's, *Réflections sur la Violence*, and Albert Camus's, *L'Homme Revolté*. The low level of campaign activity in Germany might also be associated with historical factors. Writing in the 1960s, American political scientists Gabriel Almond and Sidney Verba found that Germany lacked a *civic culture*, with participatory elements, whereas the UK, due to its history, had a well-established stable democracy. Such factors are important, yet can be overstated, and we must not assume that the UK is a haven of political tranquility. The number of UK citizens who engage in unlawful protests is almost as high as that of France despite the fact that British political culture does not value mass protest and civic unrest. Perhaps US travel writer Bill Bryson had a point when he once referred to Britain as being 'a theme-park with riots'.

Since the late 1960s in the UK several examples of *extra-parliamentary* activities have hit the headlines in this country and abroad. Extra-parliamentary politics embraces a number of activities, both legal and illegal, including demonstrations, physical obstruction, consumer boycotts, civil disobedience, petitions, riots and acts of terrorism. Examples of these activities are:

- the policy of the *National Federation for the Self-Employed* that members should withhold VAT payment to HM Customs and Excise in 1975 (civil disobedience)

- the *Countryside Alliance's* demonstrations in support of fox-hunting in 1998, 2002 and 2004

- *Greenpeace's* urged boycott of Norwegian products in protest against commercial whaling

- the *1984/85 miners' strike* (demonstrations and riots against the Conservative government's decision to close unprofitable coal mines)

- the *petrol crisis* in 2000 (physical obstruction of petrol-filling stations in protest against high fuel duties)

- the *Irish Republican Army's* bombing campaign on the British mainland from the early 1970s up to the signing of the *Good Friday Peace Agreement* in Belfast in 1998 (terrorism).

Many hypotheses have been offered to explain why citizens resort to extra-parliamentary participation. These explanations – which are not mutually exclusive – include low status, rising expectations, relative deprivation, social isolation, class, age, lack of political influence, political outlook and lack of education.

SUMMARY

- Participation and dissent are closely linked.
- Dissent and protest is a key part of political activity, which does not necessarily threaten the democratic system.
- The UK has distinctive patterns of history of participation and dissent.
- There are many explanations for protest and dissent.

3 ASSESSING POLITICAL PARTICIPATION

It is not surprising to find that campaign activity is strongly associated with citizens' attachment to a political party. People join political parties because they are interested in politics and willing to give up their free time in pursuit of the policies that their party advocates. It is almost self-evident, therefore, that such people are the most likely to be engaged in campaign activities. That they are engaged in communal activities may follow from the same tendency.

However, there are now fewer people who are members of political parties than ever before, with all major parties experiencing quite dramatic drops in membership. One single-issue pressure group, the Royal Society for the Protection of Birds (RSPB), boasts more members than all the parties put together. A staggering 98.5 per cent of UK citizens do not even belong to a political party. Trade union membership in the UK has a positive effect on the citizen's involvement in political activities, but this was not always the case. In the past – when a considerably larger number of individuals were members of trade unions (in part because employers were not able to hire employees who were not unionized; there was a so-called 'closed shop') – members of trade unions were not more politically active than their fellow workers. This has changed since the reforms of the trade union laws under the Thatcher governments in the 1980s. Since then, union membership has been associated with political interest. Union members are more likely to be members of political parties and to engage in campaign activities. However, they are less likely to be engaged in protest, perhaps because they voice their concerns through more organized channels.

It used to be a truism that younger people were more likely to participate in political protests than were older citizens. The James Dean movie *Rebel Without a Cause* (1955) was not about pensioners! Yet, it has been suggested that the generation involved in the student protests in the 1960s and the 1970s would continue taking to the streets to voice their concern and occasional outrage. (It might be that James Dean's contemporaries continued their habits when they grew older!) We do not have comparative figures between the different years, yet the current figures suggest that as citizens age their appetite for protest declines. It is, then, perhaps less surprising that older citizens are engaged in campaign activities (more older than younger citizens are members of political parties).

It seems distinctly unsurprising that the level of education is a strong predictor of political involvement in citizen politics. The more educated the individual, the higher the probability that they become engaged in political action. This has increased in recent years. There has been a move away from traditional politics dealing with materialist issues (such as social welfare and housing) towards so-called post-materialist issues, such as quality of life issues (**Lewis, 2005**). The latter require a modicum of technical knowledge about such matters as ecology, global warming and greenhouse gas emissions, which individuals with a higher education are more likely to have. Hence the tendency that more educated people are more active. This tendency perhaps explains why education is a strong predictor of activity across all forms of citizen participation. The best educated individuals are not only most likely to be engaged in political campaigns and communal meetings, but are also more likely to be engaged in protest politics. Demonstrations are not, it would seem, entirely the prerogative of the underprivileged, but are often the preserve of the better educated. Again, politics is not an exact science: in Northern Ireland, for instance, citizens with the lowest level of education tend to participate more than the educated middle-classes.

While there are only small differences in participation between the sexes, it is perhaps noteworthy that men tend to be more engaged in protest than women. Yet, women are now slightly more likely to be engaged in campaign activities and communal activities than was previously the case. These categories, however, cover a broad range of activities. The stereotypical middle-class woman preparing sandwiches for the local Conservative Club is as much engaged in a campaign activity as is her husband handing out leaflets. Moreover, the differences between the sexes are small.

Finally, it is perhaps not surprising that the least satisfied voters are more likely to participate in citizen protest. Protest, after all, is about showing dissatisfaction. What may be even more surprising is that the least satisfied are also more likely to participate in campaign and communal activities (and sometimes feel the need to do so in very extreme ways, see Box 3.1). Citizens, it would seem, do not give up on politics because they are dissatisfied – rather, they participate. This is not an altogether British finding. For example, a similar tendency can be detected in France where political dissatisfaction is even more strongly associated with political protest.

BOX 3.1   **The UK and terrorism: participation or dissent?**

Terrorism is not confined to spectacular events such as the 9-11 attack on the World Trade Center or suicide bombers in the Middle East. Until the mid 1990s, due in large measure to the actions of the IRA, terrorism was a very real part of everyday life in Northern Ireland and other parts of the UK. The story of the conflict in Northern Ireland is an example of how, when and why people sometimes resort to terrorism.

After the 1922 partition of Ireland the Unionist majority of Northern Ireland was able to govern the province as a de facto one-party state. In doing so they arguably discriminated against the interests of the – largely Catholic – Nationalists. Following growing tension between the two groups in the 1960s, a number of measures were introduced to reduce the discrimination against Nationalist citizens. This led to discontent among Unionists, who resorted to violence against the Nationalists. After more than a hundred Nationalist homes had been destroyed in 1969, the IRA re-emerged. While the IRA had existed since the Irish struggle for independence, its leadership had consisted of moderates. Things changed when militants assumed the leadership of the organization. Through armed attacks on citizens and the state, the IRA sought to achieve Irish unity. When these attacks failed to bring about the desired effect, the IRA began a bombing campaign on mainland Britain. Examples of this campaign include the killing of 19 civilians in Birmingham in November 1974 and an attempt to kill then Prime Minister Margaret Thatcher in the autumn of 1984 in the Brighton bombing. From the early 1970s to the mid 1990s a total of 3600 people were killed in the conflict. The IRA, together with other Nationalist terror groups, killed more than 1800 people (of which only 465 were British soldiers). While the IRA killed the largest number of civilians, Loyalist paramilitaries (the Unionist terror groups) killed over 980 civilians, most of them targeted Catholics.

On 31 August 1994 the IRA declared a 'complete and unequivocal' ceasefire, which was reciprocated by Loyalists a month later. This cessation of violence was prompted by the IRA's failure to counter the Loyalist paramilitaries' increasingly successful attacks, by dwindling public support for *armed struggle*, and by the decision of key Republicans to abandon a military strategy in favour of a political campaign for Irish unity. It was not only the IRA, but also the governments of the Republic of Ireland and the UK, that realized the ongoing war was both futile and costly. Of great symbolic importance was the declaration of the British Secretary of State for Northern Ireland, Peter Brooke, that Britain had no 'selfish, strategic or economic interest in Northern Ireland'. The agreement of the Irish and British governments to let the people of Northern Ireland decide their own future, to govern themselves by sharing power, further undermined the rationale for the armed struggle. It prompted the peace process and led to the signing of the Good Friday Peace Agreement in 1998. While the political situation in Northern Ireland remains somewhat unstable, much has changed since the early 1970s and the peace process continues to slowly edge forward, if occasionally taking some steps backward. Whether the IRA's armed struggle against the British government was conducive to bringing about this change is a matter of some contention. Similar questions may be asked about the human costs of the 'long war'. Did the 3600 plus people whose lives were sacrificed during the conflict die in vain? Or were the human costs justified? Indeed, can terrorist acts ever be justified?

(based on McGarry and O'Leary, 1995; see also Chapter 2)

But should UK citizens participate more? Many reformers stress that participation is often an end in itself. Some political reformers have, consequently, sought to encourage such virtuous activity, for example through schemes such as so-called tele-voting and Internet voting.

Let's consider the argument that holding more referendums in the UK would prompt a positive increase in political participation.

Although only one national referendum has ever been held (in June 1975, on EU membership; Figure 3.1), referendums have been increasingly used in the UK, on Welsh and Scottish devolution, the Northern Ireland peace process, the introduction of a government for London and for local mayors, and on possible future entry into the European single currency. Referendums were once viewed as 'unconstitutional', but now politicians have began to submit certain policy issues to the electorate. Some believe that this trend marks a new tendency towards growing citizen involvement in politics. The process of submitting issues to the voters, means that they – not elected politicians – are allowed to have the last word.

FIGURE 3.1 Margaret Thatcher, then Leader of the Opposition, with three pro-Market campaigners, London, 1975

However, it is sometimes questionable whether referendums are called in an attempt to boost citizen participation. Referendums may be a convenient way of resolving an internal dispute within a governing party. For instance, unable to find common ground on the issue of membership of the EU in the 1970s, the Labour Party resorted to asking citizens, in a referendum, if they wished the UK to remain in the EU. Moreover, while a referendum enables the voters to have a say on a policy issue, politicians are unlikely to submit an issue to a referendum if they think they will not get the outcome they hope for.

A referendum is often called to generate support for the government, not to threaten the government. The political philosopher Michael Oakeshott summed up the latter view: 'The plebiscite [referendum] is not a method by which mass man [*sic*] imposes his choices upon his rulers, it is a method for generating a government with unlimited authority to make choices on his behalf. In the plebiscite, mass man achieved final release from the burden of individuality. He was emphatically told what to choose' (Oakeshott, 1991, p.38). Perhaps so, yet the fact that the voters have occasionally rejected the government's recommendations might suggest an alternative interpretation.

In general, the more highly educated the individual, the higher their levels of participation. In Northern Ireland, however, where lower education produces higher participation, the relationship seems to be the opposite. Political science needs to pay attention to such differences – to have a keen eye for the general trends, but also a sense for the specific factors.

Elections do not function solely as a means of selecting the political elite, as is sometimes assumed. They also have a 'signalling effect'. Many vote for a political party to ensure it forms a government which will enact and implement desired policies. However, these 'instrumentalist' voters are not alone. Other voters – while not oblivious to instrumentalist concerns – may display their disagreement with the political system and the political debate by voting for fringe, protest and single-issue parties. This is not necessarily because they believe, hope or expect that such parties will form a government, but because they wish to register dissent with a political system that exclusively focuses on material issues. The same logic may explain why there is some support for the Monster Raving Loony Party, the British National Party, the UK Independence Party, the Referendum Party and also single-issue candidates. A vote for one of these parties or an individual candidate, such as ex-BBC journalist Martin Bell (elected in the Tatton constituency on an anti-sleaze platform in 1997), may therefore send a signal to the major parties that certain issues are not being addressed satisfactorily.

In 1997, Sir James Goldsmith, a millionaire businessman, formed the Referendum Party with the sole aim of ensuring that a future referendum would be held should the government recommend joining the European single currency. It had no policy other than this (although it displayed a general antipathy and hostility to the EU) and drew upon support from the right as well as from the left. While the Referendum Party did not succeed in having any MPs elected, both Labour and the Conservatives adopted the referendum policy and included a manifesto pledge to hold a referendum in the event of a decision to join the euro (Qvortrup, 2002, p.116).

While participation is often seen as an ideal, some scholars argue that citizens, by exhausting their civic reserves, will not have any resources for mobilizing when really critical issues emerge. We have seen that citizens may sometimes feel that they 'have to' resort to extra-parliamentary politics, particularly when traditional means of influencing politicians fail (or are deemed inadequate).

The existence of these different forms of participation raises other questions: when and why do people get involved in politics?

- Citizens' participation varies significantly according to, among other things, education, age, gender, political identification, political affiliation, union membership and political satisfaction.
- While participation may be a 'good thing', too much activity could create 'political fatigue'.
- Devices that may increase participation in the UK, such as the referendum, may not always have the intended effects.
- Some parties/candidates come forward in order to register dissent or protest.

4 CITIZENS AS VOTERS: PARTY IDENTIFICATION

As we have seen, voting is not the only form of political participation – many people participate but do not vote. Although democracy is impossible without free elections and voting is ultimately seen as the litmus test of democracy, participation is not the main indicator of how democratic a regime is – indeed, many authoritarian states have actively encouraged participation. With elections at the centre of democratic activity, why do turnout rates seem to show a downward trend? The traditional belief was that a low level of participation could be explained by a lack of education and membership of one of the lower social classes. Yet, as membership of the working classes shrinks and levels of education rise, electoral turnout continues to dwindle. **Lewis (2005)** and **Smith (2005)** have discussed this trend; here, I dig further into issues of party identification and changes in the UK context.

There are numerous competing theories explaining low levels of electoral participation. For many, declining participation is explained by political, not social, factors (Butler and Stokes, 1974). Turnout goes up and down depending on how exciting (or otherwise) electors find the campaign. Central to this theory is the concept of *party identification*. Voters are often socialized to identify with one of the two major political parties, Labour or the Conservatives, but this is not always the case. Citizens who identify with a party – party identifiers – not only have a tendency to vote in every election, but tend to vote for their preferred party. Non-party identifiers, by contrast, will tend not to vote unless they are prompted to do so by short-term factors. The Michigan School – which is credited with the invention of this model – identified three kinds of elections:

- maintaining elections
- deviating elections
- re-aligning elections.

In a 'maintaining election' the outcome will be decided by party identifiers. Thus the party with the highest number of party identifiers will tend to win. This is not so in a 'deviating election'; here, the non-party identifiers will be prompted to vote (thus increasing turnout) for the minority party. In a deviating election the result differs from the 'normal vote', typically to the benefit of the party with the smallest number of party identifiers.

The model was originally developed for US presidential elections. Since the beginning of the 1930s a majority of the US voters had identified themselves as Democrats. In 1948, when the Democrat incumbent Harry Truman won the election, turnout was low and few issues captured the voters' imaginations. The election was a typical *maintaining election*. The result, consequently, reflected the 'normal' vote. The people who voted were the party identifiers and, because the Democrats had more party identifiers than the Republicans, they won.

In 1956, when the Republican Dwight Eisenhower was re-elected, the turnout was impressive, and the campaign was rich on short-term factors (among them the Soviet Union's invasion of Hungary and the Suez crisis). Many non-party identifiers turned out to vote, and some Democrats defected to the Republicans. The 1956 presidential election was, therefore, a *deviating election*.

Of course, there are elections which altogether alter the identification of the voters. This typically happens during a national crisis. The US presidential election in 1932 is an example of a 're-aligning election'. The Republicans had been the dominant party since the 1880s and the majority of voters were Republican Party identifiers. The election and re-election of Democrat Woodrow Wilson in 1912 and 1916 followed the usual pattern of a high turnout and many short-term factors. In 1932, however, led by Franklin Roosevelt, the Democrats succeeded in altering the electorate's party preferences for successive generations, fashioning a New Deal coalition, which supported governmental activity to combat economic depression.

Can a similar model apply in the UK context? It would depend on the distribution of partisan alignments. One would expect the Conservatives, having governed the UK for more than two-thirds of the twentieth century, to be the political party with the highest numbers of party identifiers, but this is not reflected in the distribution of party identifiers. Until the 1979 general election the Labour Party boasted the largest number of party identifiers, but was then overtaken by the Conservatives (in what might be described as a re-aligning election). We would expect that turnout would have been lowest in the years when the Labour Party won, as only committed voters are likely to turn out. In fact, it was not. Turnout was higher than the average turnout (of 75.3 per cent) in the general elections that Labour won. We would have expected turnout to surge in the election of 1970, when the Conservatives won, but it did not. Turnout dropped to 72.2 per cent. Yet, while the model does not seem to explain the outcome or turnout in all the UK elections since 1945, the 1997 and 2001 (see Figure 3.2) elections do conform to the theory. Labour won both elections, had the highest number of party identifiers, and the turnout was low. Table 3.2 (overleaf) provides turnout and party fortunes for UK elections between 1964 and 2001.

FIGURE 3.2   Michael Portillo, Conservative candidate for Kensington and Chelsea, General Election night, June 2001

Nevertheless, the model does not provide a general theory. Moreover, many *psephologists* believe that the model is past its sell-by date. (*Psephology* is a technical term for the study of election results and trends. It derives from the ancient Greek word for pebble (*psefos*): the Greeks used small pieces of pebble as 'ballot paper'.) The typology in the model not only fails to explain the turnout rate, but is also structurally undermined by the fact that the number of party identifiers is declining. This phenomenon is described as *de-alignment*, and means that the usefulness of the concept as an independent variable has declined. But what other explanations are there? Has the system itself changed perhaps?

TABLE 3.2 UK General Elections 1964–2001: turnout; party identification and winning party (percentages of electorate)

Year	Turnout (%)	Labour Party identification (%)	Conservative Party identification (%)	Winning party
1964	77.1	42	39	Labour
1966	75.8	45	36	Labour
1970	72.2	43	40	Conservative
1974	78.7	40	35	Labour
1974	72.8	40	34	Labour
1979	76.0	36	38	Conservative
1983	72.7	31	36	Conservative
1987	75.3	30	37	Conservative
1992	77.7	31	42	Conservative
1997	71.6	40	31	Labour
2001	59.9	40	28	Labour

Source: British Election Study, 1948–2001

Some critics have argued that declining turnout since 1990 is due to the electoral system, which – they argue – is unfair and a disincentive for participating. Why? As Richard Heffernan illustrates in Chapter 1, critics argue that the UK's electoral system creates disincentives for certain voters. Why should, say, a Labour voter living in a Tory constituency cast a vote when it does not make a difference to the outcome? What is the point in turning out to vote if one's vote is 'wasted'? Of course, the symbolic importance of the very act of voting should never be discounted or underestimated. Some voters may see it as a manifestation of their personal beliefs that they vote for a candidate of a party with which they associate. Whether the candidate wins is not the only thing that matters. Having heroically sought to counter a trend – or having stayed true to the party supported by one's group of peers – may be symbolically important, yet it is unlikely that large numbers of voters attach much value to the act of voting. It seems more likely that citizens will decide not to vote if their candidate has no chance of winning. See also Box 3.2.

BOX 3.2   **The paradox of voting**

Some theorists think it is a paradox that citizens bother to vote at all when their personal gain is so small and the chance their vote will be decisive is minimal. Have you ever wondered why people bother to vote, when the chance that they will cast the decisive vote is minimal? Anthony Downs devoted a book to the subject (Downs, 1957) and concluded that it was economically irrational to vote. Here is his argument.

Suppose there are two parties contesting an election. One party proposes a tax increase of one per cent. The other party does not advocate a tax increase. You favour the latter, but you are only one of several million voters. Your failure to cast your vote is unlikely to decide the outcome of the election. Moreover, taking a day off work and making your way to the polling station is a bit of hassle. Given the minimal personal advantage you can gain from voting – and the cost of acquiring the information you need to vote – it is surprising that people bother to vote at all. Particularly so, when there is only a chance of one in 28 million (in the UK) that you will cast the decisive vote.

Yet many – indeed a majority – of citizens do vote. Some would argue that people vote because they feel that this is their civic duty. Try to consider if you find it rational to vote. Do you vote? Why – or why not? Is it a paradox that people vote? Many proponents of *rational choice theory* believe voting is irrational and some political scientists of a more qualitative and historical persuasion tend to agree.

However, British citizens are comparatively just as active as their German and French counterparts, yet turnout in Britain is below that of Germany. The USA has always had comparatively low turnouts in federal elections, but Britain did enjoy much higher levels than the 59 per cent recorded in the 2001 general election (Table 3.2). **Smith (2005)** sets out the main types of electoral systems, such as additional member system (AMS). As Table 3.3 (overleaf) suggests, turnout in countries with proportional representation (PR) is higher than in countries with single member plurality systems (SMPS). (The other abbreviation in the table is STV for single transferable vote.)

There is not, however, a neat relationship between turnout and electoral system. Switzerland, which has a PR party list system, has one of the lowest turnout rates in the West. Moreover, in spite of the proportionality of the electoral system used there, the turnout rate in Ireland is among the lowest. The turnout in the UK might have dropped in recent years, yet its post-1945 average turnout is actually among the highest in the advanced industrial world. Institutional factors alone clearly cannot explain turnout, because historical and social factors need to be taken into account as well.

TABLE 3.3 Turnout rates in Western democracies

Country	PR	Electoral system	Turnout rate (1950–2000)
Austria	PR	party list	84
Canada		SMPS	69
Denmark	PR	party list	83
Finland	PR	party list	72
France		majoritarian second ballot	69
Germany		AMS	77
Greece	PR	party list	80
Iceland	PR	party list	88
Republic of Ireland	PR	STV	66
Luxembourg	PR	party list	87
Netherlands	PR	party list	78
New Zealand		AMS	80
Norway	PR	party list	76
Portugal	PR	party list	68
Spain	PR	party list	76
Sweden	PR	party list	87
Switzerland	PR	party list	46
UK		SMPS	78
USA		SMPS	53

Countries with compulsory voting, such as Australia and Belgium, are not included.
Source: adapted from Dalton, 1996

SUMMARY

- There are three main types of elections: maintaining, deviating and aligning.

- These types have much to do with party identification.

- Turn-out at elections varies across countries, but has declined significantly between 1990 and 2001 in the UK.

- The model developed by the Michigan School has been an influential one in attempts to explain why people vote.

- No simple correlation between turnout and type of electoral system has been identified; some theories argue that voting is an irrational activity.

5 RECENT THEORIES OF ELECTORAL CHOICE: CLASS VOTING AND ITS ALTERNATIVES

'Class', it was once said, 'is the basis of British party politics. All else is embellishment and detail' (Pulzer, 1967, p.98); but not all observers agree. We have seen how non-class social movements have introduced new forms of political participation in the UK and elsewhere (**Smith, 2005**). Here, I focus on class voting transformation in the UK.

5.1   The traditional model

Some have declared class in UK party politics to be an obsolete concept, others have made a case for revision of the way in which class is defined and measured. Class is a common enough concept. Yet, agreeing on a definition of 'class' is easier said than done. Marx and Engels, writing in 1848, were among the first to use the concept in a way recognizable today; they believed that 'society as a whole is more and more splitting up into two great hostile camps, into two great classes facing each other' (Marx and Engels, 1985, p.80). Contemporary sociologists specializing in social stratification – whether Marxists or not – now believe that society is considerably more complex than Marx and Engels believed. While there is an abundance of systems for social stratification and class membership, most sociologists and political scientists focus on six categories of occupations:

A   *higher professional, managerial and administrative*
   e.g. barristers, physicians, company directors, senior civil servants

B   *intermediate professional, managerial and administrative*
   e.g. university lecturers, teachers, junior executives

C1 *supervisor, clerical and other non-manual*
   e.g. secretaries, bank tellers, police sergeants

C2 *skilled manual*
   e.g. electricians, machinists

D   *semi-skilled and unskilled manual*
   e.g. factory fitters, bus conductors

E   *residual, casual workers, people on state benefits*
   e.g. pensioners and the unemployed.

While this categorization would indicate that the dichotomous model of the class antagonism is overly simplistic, some have sought to divide the six categories into two. The first three categories (A–C1) can be described as the middle classes, while (C2–E) may be said to comprise the working classes. Based on this categorization, political scientists have sought to determine if class remains a predictor of voting behaviour.

Some influential sociologists have argued that class has ceased to be an important variable. US sociologist Ronald Inglehart finds that 'the shift towards post modern values has brought ... a shift from political cleavages based on social class conflict towards cleavages based on cultural issues and quality of life concerns' (Inglehart, 1997, p.237). But has class ceased to be a reliable predictor of electoral choice? Robert Alford, another US sociologist, has sought to develop a measure of the importance of 'class voting'. The UK Alford measure, the Alford Index of Class-Voting, is statistically simple; it is found by subtracting the Labour Party's percentage share of the vote among non-manual workers (A–C1) from that of Labour's share among manual workers (C2–E). Thus if 20 per cent of the middle-class voters vote for this party, the Alford Index of Class Voting will be 80 − 20 = 60.

Since the Second World War, figures have consistently shown that the Alford Index has fallen, but that the fall has been uneven. The Alford-Index, close to 50 in the 1940s, is presently steady at about 10. This indicates a growing importance of middle-class voters to Labour and the reduced importance of working-class voters. This result has come about as a result of Conservative inroads among C2 voters, often referred to as 'Essex man', in the 1980s. It has also been encouraged by the increasing propensity to vote Labour among professionals and the middle classes. These figures – if read in isolation – would indicate the emergence of 'catch-all parties' (parties that seek support from all sections of society, not simply specific groups of voters) and demonstrate the decline of class-based voting. Clearly, political parties no longer seek the support of distinct groups in society as in the past. Instead, they seek support from all segments in society. No longer a party only of and for the working classes, the Labour Party seeks to attract middle-class voters; in this regard, it is defiantly 'New Labour'.

There is something intuitively convincing about this argument. UK society has changed – and class structures have changed with it. The working world of the 1950s, steel mills, coalmines and manufacturing industry, has gone. The UK today bears all the hallmarks of post-industrial society; streets crowded with building societies, fast-food chains and an increasing proportion of the population working in the service sector. In 1971, roughly 50 per cent of all males were working in the manufacturing industry, but by 2000 this figure had dropped to 33 per cent. These changes not only altered society, but also rendered obsolete the traditional models of social stratification. The traditional six-fold division was no longer analytically useful as a predictor of social attitudes. In a much cited book, sociologist John Goldthorpe proposed a new, five-fold, division of society which incorporated an occupation's degree of economic security, authority in the work place and levels of income, rather than the perceived social status of the 1950s (Goldthorpe, 1980). The categories were: the Salariat; Routine Manual Workers, the Petty Bourgeoisie, Foreman and Technicians; and the Working Class. These societal changes challenge Pulzer's assertion from the 1960s. If class is no longer as significant a social variable as it once was, how then can class have a continuing impact on voting behaviour and electoral politics?

5.2 The 'revisionist' alternative

By the mid 1980s a number of political scientists found that working-class voting had all but ceased to be a valuable predictor of citizens' voting behaviour. Not all agreed with this, however. While nobody sought to resurrect the 'orthodox' model (which suggested that economic class determined the way citizens vote), some political sociologists made a case for what has become known as the 'revisionist' theory of class voting. Here, Anthony Heath, John Curtice and Roger Jowell argued that there had been no class de-alignment (Heath *et al.*, 1985). While they conceded that class sizes had changed since the early 1960s, they claimed that relative class voting had not. The same proportion of workers continued to vote for the Labour Party. However, the size of this group had shrunk. Hence the appearance of declining class voting.

There has been considerable debate about this revisionist theory. While the traditional – or Marxist – model of class antagonism appears of limited analytical value, such research seems to suggest that the rumours of the demise of class voting are exaggerated. One's socio-economic position in society can still be a predictor of one's political attitudes and behaviour. Nevertheless, it is no longer the case that society is splitting into two antagonized camps.

Class voting and the Michigan model may be described as structural theories. Here, it is assumed that structures – be they as socialization, class or occupation – determine (or at least influence) the citizen's political attitude and electoral behaviour. There need not be anything automatic in this. Class may be an important predictor of electoral behaviour, because voters find it rational to vote for a political party that fights for their interests. In the twentieth century, working-class people undoubtedly supported the Labour Party for economic reasons; Labour would be more likely to improve their well-being, whereas the Conservatives were less likely to do so.

Yet, as a general rule, the premise of such models is that voters do not base their political behaviour on rational considerations, let alone on political issues, but it is precisely these latter concepts that lie at the heart of alternative theories of electoral and political behaviour, particularly 'issue voting' and 'rational choice' models of voting. As in the case of the Michigan model, the inspiration for alternative theories were imported from the USA.

5.3 The 'economic voting' model as an example of issue voting

The Michigan model had painted a rather bleak picture of the voter as a socialized individual, who would, apparently without reflection, vote for a political party. This model – while inconsistent with the basic premise of democratic theory – was supported by survey evidence in the 1940s and 1950s, but the picture seemingly changed in the 1960s. In the USA, growing political discontent, student revolt, increased political awareness and a growing importance of issues led several political scientists to revise the traditional models of electoral behaviour. Many found evidence of a considerable political sophistication on the part of many electors. This sophistication was shared – albeit with a slightly different focus – by proponents of so-called economic voting.

The theory of economic voting, like that of 'issue voting', was inspired by other US-based research. In 1966, V.O. Key, a Texan political scientist, advanced what he called the 'perverse and unorthodox theory that voters are not fools, they appraise past performances and past actions' (Key, 1966, p.7). His study, however, was not clad in sophisticated statistical models, although such models have subsequently become the hallmark of the approach. Key's significance lay in instituting a paradigm based on 'retrospective voting'. Yet, unlike Key, most of his followers have based their models on economic issues. Voters, it is argued, consider the Government's macro-economic record, and base their electoral choice on their retrospective evaluation of its performance. The theory of economic voting is a US invention, which has spread to the UK in recent years. One of the most impressive examples of the model's ability to predict elections is provided by British political scientist David Sanders's correct prediction that the Conservative Party in the UK would win the 1992 general election, when opinion polls suggested that Labour would win (Butler and Kavanagh, 1993). By using a figure called the 'feel-good factor', a measure of the voters' confidence in their own economic fortunes, Sanders predicted the outcome of the election. The model was also used to explain the Conservative's defeat in 1997. Whether this model is merely based on a lucky guess remains to be seen. Some would perhaps argue that the economic voting model fails to explain the underlying causes of electoral behaviour. Yet this model (as with each of the other models) should not be seen in isolation. The various models of electoral behaviour complement each other – they are not necessarily alternatives.

S U M M A R Y

- There are several different explanations of why citizens make electoral choices: the Michigan model, models of class voting, issue voting, and retrospective 'economic' voting.

- There is considerable interest in the emergence of new concepts, such as issue voting, which prompt notions such as de-alignment, the idea that citizens can readily abandon past electoral allegiances.

- We know a great deal about elections – and about why people cast their votes. Yet, new questions continue to emerge.

6 FRAMING PUBLIC OPINION: THE MASS MEDIA, POLITICAL PARTICIPATION AND SPIN

'The people is never corrupted, but is often deceived, and on such occasions only does it seem to will what is bad' (Rousseau, 1913, p.23). Jean-Jacques Rousseau's assessment of the citizens' propensity to be lured into voting for politicians and policies (to which, in reality, they were opposed) seems to resonate with recent developments in UK politics – not least with the apparent power of the press and so-called 'spin'.

6.1 Role of the mass media

The Labour Party – including Tony Blair himself – was at pains to win the support of *The Sun* newspaper in 1997. Perhaps understandably, the party wanted to prevent a repetition of the 1992 general election in which it was argued that *The Sun* helped John Major to a fourth consecutive Conservative victory. Following a personalized campaign against the then Labour leader Neil Kinnock, the paper took credit for the Labour Party's defeat with the front-page headline 'It was the Sun wot won it'.

Anxious to prevent another Tory victory, Blair actively courted the paper's proprietor Rupert Murdoch, and succeeded in shifting *The Sun* into the Labour camp. Psephologists are not entirely convinced that *The Sun* played a crucial role. Although Labour secured the paper's backing, the party did not gain any more votes after *The Sun*'s decision to back Blair.

This fact seems to indicate that Labour gained little from winning over Murdoch. Yet, it is possible that securing his support worked in a more subtle fashion. While the net result may have seemed meagre – indeed non-existent – it is possible that Labour influenced *Sun* readers, but did not win the support of the readers of other newspapers. To determine the effect of *The Sun*'s support on the Labour Party's fortunes in 1997 requires a microanalysis of individual voters' attitudes and voting decisions. We are particularly interested in finding out if readers of *The Sun* newspaper were more prone to switch to Labour during the campaign and if the readers of other traditional supporters of the Conservatives, such as the *Daily Mail, Daily Telegraph* and *Daily Express*, also followed the Labour bandwagon. We can get an indication of this from the data shown in Table 3.4.

TABLE 3.4   The 1997 electoral campaign: voters' responses to *The Sun*'s decision to back Labour

Paper read regularly	Probablility of change (%)		
	Conservative	Labour	Liberal Democrat
Tory faithful	+1	−4	+5
The Sun	−6	+1	+0
Labour faithful	+1	−11	+3

The table shows the probability that voters changed their decision to vote after having read one of the newspapers that advocated a particular political party. For example, a *Sun* reader who had said she would vote Conservative a year before the election would be six per cent less likely to do so as a result of *The Sun*'s decision to back Labour.
Source: British Election Study, 1997

The table seems to indicate that the Conservatives increased their support among readers of Conservative-supporting newspapers, whereas Labour was unable to make net gains among these voters (first row). The data also indicate that *The Sun* improved the Labour Party's fortunes (second row). The Conservatives had lost support from *The Sun* readers (−6), whereas the Labour Party seems to have gained somewhat, albeit not much (+1). However, this gain was offset by the considerable drop in the number of voters reading the Labour-faithful newspapers (third row). Compared with the year before the election, the Labour Party dropped by 11 points among the readers of the paper that had supported Blair all along. It was not *The Sun* 'wot won it' in 1997. In fact, one might speculate that the Labour Party would not have lost quite so many supporters had they not courted the traditional Conservative press.

While the table thus indicates that *The Sun* modestly improved Labour's standing, the data do not provide any explanation for why the Liberal Democrats were able to improve their standing among all groups – except among *Sun* readers (last column). No newspaper supported the Liberal Democrats (though *The Independent* and *The Observer* urged their voters to vote tactically for the party with the best chance of beating the Conservative candidate). If the media determined the electoral choice of its readers then surely we would have expected the Liberal Democrats to have lost votes, whereas in fact they gained them.

This result suggests that the media's role is somewhat dramatized, not least by the media themselves. Because they play a key role in the dissemination of political news, the mass media are important players in politics. However, most analysts of public opinion do not believe that the media tell voters what to think and how to vote. The media seem to have an *agenda-setting function.* Not being able to tell voters *what to think* – as alleged in the Rousseau quote – they can influence what the voters *think about.* This is a considerable influence. By focusing the agenda on issues that favour one party rather than another, the media may thereby indirectly influence the outcome of elections. There is, however, little direct survey evidence that supports this hypothesis in the UK. Given the numerous influences that help determine how electors vote, the role of the media, as only one influencing medium among many, remains disputed.

6.2 How public opinion is organized: the politics of spin doctors

'Events, dear boy, events' was Conservative Prime Minister Harold Macmillan's reply to a question regarding what determined the popularity of a government. This is as true today as it was in the 1950s. Public opinion can be volatile; a single event can turn public opinion and affect the fortune of the government. For instance, more or less spontaneous protests against the price of fuel in September 2000 led to a temporary shift in public opinion. Governments – and opposition parties – will try to defend themselves from criticisms and to present their own policies in the best light possible. However, there are indications that politicians in recent years have become more aware of presentational issues – often called spin – than was previously the case.

In recent years the political vocabulary has been extended by terms such as 'spin doctors', 'sound bites' and 'focus groups'. Alastair Campbell, Tony Blair's former press spokesperson and director of communications, Peter Mandelson, the former Cabinet Minister, and Philip Gould, Blair's current adviser (who conducts polls for the prime minister), have all been accused of using news media management to manipulate and control public opinion. Has presentation become more important than substance? And can 'spin' lure voters? How – if at all – can public opinion be shaped? What do spin doctors do? What is designer politics?

In the days of class politics, matters were said to be simple. Each party represented a group or class in society, which aggregated and formulated policies, articulated by interest organizations that spoke for the ordinary members. In the case of the Labour party, the policies originated from the trade unions. A higher proportion of citizens were members of political parties. In short, it was comparatively easy for political parties to formulate ideas; they could rely on the individual members and organizations. This is no longer the case. The membership of political parties has declined, so much so that, by way of comparison, the combined membership of all political parties is now lower that the total membership of the RSPB.

This poses a problem for all political parties. No longer able to formulate policies on the basis of demand from ordinary party members, political parties are forced to look elsewhere for policy ideas – and for assessment of policies. Political parties can now – crudely speaking – choose between one of two options. They can adopt an ideological stance (and hope that enough electors agree with them), or they can design a policy on the basis of what it is deemed that the electorate want. The latter is what is meant by *designer politics*, which is based on the premise that it is possible for a party to engineer policies that suit the electorate with the objective of thereby attracting votes. Yet what does the electorate think? And can it be discovered if policies really suit the voters? Parties use opinion polls and focus groups to try to find out what the electorate like and dislike (and to road test their ideas). Political parties conduct a series of benchmark polls, that is, opinion polls which ask respondents about their general political attitudes and try to assess their feeling towards the parties. This information is correlated with personal typologies, particularly age, gender, occupation, education and geographical location, to construct an impression of electoral opinion and to track changes in those opinions. Subsequent polls try to determine developments in the party's progress by mapping out electoral attitudes towards ongoing campaigns.

On the basis of benchmark polls, parties attempt to identify policies that suit the electorate. Such policies are tested in small focus groups, groups of voters (typically 6–12 people) who are asked to discuss a proposal, a poster or an idea. Sometimes the discussion is watched from behind a screen, sometimes a facilitator takes notes, and sometimes the discussion is recorded. The aim of setting up the focus group is to record the public's assessment of policies. It is not enough that a political party adopts a new image, which is supported by the majority of the voters, because the party must be seen to be a credible exponent for the policy. This is not automatically the case. Under the leadership of William Hague the Conservative Party attempted to modernize itself by adopting a new image. This may have been more consistent with voters' preferences, but the Conservatives were not widely considered to be credible deliverers of the new message (Lees-Marshment and Quayle, 2001).

Having assessed public attitudes the political party is then ready to launch the policy, but this is not always straightforward. Party officials charged with news media relations, the spin doctors, seek to feed their particular angle – their take on the policy – to the news media, with the intention of influencing how the story runs. Selected journalists may be offered the story (possibly with the expectation that they will provide favourable coverage) and discreet lobbying will take place to construct the news agenda in a way that favours the party and brings it supportive coverage. Of course, the news media, which prides itself on its political independence, is often ready and able to evaluate and interrogate a party's policy, so the interrelationship between the party and the news media is often as conflictual as it is supportive. In addition, other parties will not, however, be idle, seeking to challenge their opponents' policies, more usually by deploying so-called rebuttal strategies. Party officials collect files and facts on other parties in order to attack their policies, outlining, say, the 'real' consequences and the alleged 'hidden costs' involved.

While these strategies are increasingly used, it remains an open question how effective they are. Rick Ridder, a professional campaigner, has estimated that a campaign can 'at best win up to five per cent. You cannot turn an awful candidate into a good one. You can minimize damage' (Ridder, 2003). Whatever the effects, however, political parties can't afford not to use these tactics. The risk that another party's more persuasive campaign could cost them the campaign is too great. Hence the growing use of designer politics – even at a time when political parties are strapped for cash.

As is always the case, many critics decry the effects of designer politics (Figure 3.3). This is nothing new. Designer politics has characterized all forms of democratic government. The methods may change, yet all politicians have occasionally resorted to designer politics to win the argument. The Athenian philosopher Plato (428–348 BC) in his *Protagonas* raged against the so-called 'Sophists', the professional teachers who taught budding politicians to convince their audience. While much has changed since the days of Athenian democracy, some things have stayed the same.

FIGURE 3.3   'In a spin' – Blair's televised briefings to end spin

Yet, this association does not rob the modern day *sophistry* of democratic legitimacy. Plato was famously opposed to democracy; the sophists were not. At one level, the sophists were merely helping the politicians to communicate better. Many suggest that designer politics merely helps politicians pick up the views of the citizens at a time when the political parties no longer speak directly for citizens. As such, designer politics provides a link between the elite and the people, which previously was provided by the political parties.

Some would undoubtedly prefer that this function be transferred back to the political parties. The parties had a socializing function, something necessary for any democracy, when party members (and would-be supporters) took an interest in political issues. In contrast, ordinary citizens do not deliberate when asked a couple of questions by a pollster, but they are more representative of the population as a whole. The members of political parties are more likely to be more middle class, white and urban than the population as a whole. Moreover, they are likely to hold more extreme views. By relying on the views of party members, political parties are more likely to develop policies that are inconsistent with the views of the voters as a whole. When relying on the views of the citizens as interviewed in mass surveys and focus groups, parties are more likely to represent a moderated, middle-of-the-road position. Of course, whether that is desirable is an open question.

So, political participation – whether organized or not – is sometimes influenced by factors other than ideological beliefs and social and economic interest. The question of free will is not just a matter for philosophers. The news media, so-called designer politics, and the politics of news management and spin, are influential as well.

SUMMARY

- The media can have some – albeit limited – effect on voters' electoral choices.

- The media's influence may relate more to agenda setting than to voters' electoral choices.

- Designer politics illustrates that political parties and candidates seek to gauge the views and opinions of the voters and tailor their policies accordingly. Designer politics, news management and spin seem to be an integral part of democratic politics – for better or for worse.

7 CONCLUSION

The average citizen, argues a political strategist, 'spends a mere twelve minutes a year discussing politics' (Ridder, 2003), although there is no empirical confirmation of this assessment. Figures indicate that, while politics does not occupy their entire life, UK citizens are fairly involved in politics. A majority of citizens vote in general elections (although a smaller majority than was previously the case) and significant numbers are engaged in campaigns, communal activities and in other ways of making their political concerns heard.

Their involvement is caused by a variety of factors. Educational attainment remains the best predictor of political activity, if not of political outlook. The increase in education has led to a growing increase in political involvement, in spite of a declining electoral turnout since 1990. It is suggested by some that this decline is a matter of concern, because it is caused by either political apathy, declining 'social capital' or by the break-up of hitherto existing party loyalties. Others maintain that the drop in turnout reflects a growing distrust in an electoral system that enables a party to win a majority of seats in the House of Commons without a majority of the votes. Neither of these theories is flawless, but neither is without some merit. Political science is not an exact science, the reasons why citizens participate are varied, but several distinct patterns can be discerned.

The same may be said of citizens' electoral behaviour. Class is not what it used to be. Society may no longer be split into two antagonistic classes, but class has not entirely ceased to be a predictor for how some individuals cast their ballots. Working-class citizens continue to support the Labour Party in greater numbers than support the Conservative Party. But voting is no longer determined only by class, and it is questionable if class alone ever determined it. Issues – not least economic issues – are increasingly important in politics. While economic conditions cannot explain all aspects of electoral outcomes, it is nevertheless noteworthy that some analysts have had considerable success predicting the outcome of elections by using economic figures.

Does this trend supersede traditional explanations, such as the alleged role of the news media? The role of the press was at any rate always disputed. The view that the press could influence voters' electoral behaviour has been qualified many times. No consensus has emerged, however, and many scholars (perhaps even a majority) have argued that all forms of the media, broadcast news and print journalism alike, have only an agenda-setting function: unable to tell voters what to think, but able to tell them what to think about. While the press does not decide elections, it has occasionally happened that a newspaper, by supporting a particular party, can impact upon the voting intentions of its readers.

If the persuading influence of the press is limited, it is perhaps surprising that political parties increasingly resort to designer politics to win elections – if newspaper articles cannot change the voters' minds, why should advertisements? There are not many studies of the effect of designer politics, so why resort to this expensive means of convincing voters? The reasons may be structural. With the decline in party membership – and with parties being increasingly divorced from the traditional hinterland of interest organizations – political parties no longer get direct input from members and sympathizers. This lack of policy input has forced political parties to seek new ways of gauging the voters' demands and attitudes. Political parties and candidates seek to do this using public opinion surveys and focus groups. Whether this trend will prove detrimental to political participation and citizen politics remains to be seen.

Finally, we should also remember that those orthodox methods of engaging with politics and participation do not exhaust the methods of political expression. Dissent and extra-parliamentary activity remain as important in giving vent to political opinions as are voting and taking part in focus groups.

REFERENCES

Butler, D. and Kavanagh, D. (1993) *The British General Election in 1992*, London, Macmillan.

Butler, D. and Stokes, D. (1974) *Political Change in Britain*, London, Macmillan.

Dalton, R.J. (1996) *Citizen Politics: Public Opinion and Political Parties in Advanced Industrial Democracies* (2nd edn), New York, Chatham House.

Downs, A. (1957) *An Economic Theory of Democracy*, New York, Harper Row.

Goldthorpe, J.H. (1980) *Social Mobility and Class Structure in Modern Britain*, Oxford, Oxford University Press.

Heath, A., Curtice, J. and Jowell, R. (1985) *How Britain Votes*, Oxford, Oxford University Press.

Inglehart, R. (1997) *Modernization and Post-modernization: Cultural, Economic and Political Change in 43 Countries*, Princeton, Princeton University Press.

Key, V.O. (1966) *The Responsible Electorate*, Cambridge, MA, Belknap Press.

Lees-Marshment, J. and Quayle, S. (2001) 'Empowering the members or marketing the party? The Conservative reforms of 1998', *The Political Quarterly*, vol.72, no.2, April–June.

Lewis, P.G. (2005) 'Politics, powers and structures' in Lewis, P.G. (ed.) *Exploring Political Worlds*, Edinburgh, Edinburgh University Press/The Open University.

McGarry, J. and O'Leary, B. (1995) *The Politics of Antagonism: Interpreting Northern Ireland*, Oxford, Blackwell.

Marx, K. and Engels, F. (1985) *The Communist Manifesto*, London, Penguin.

Oakeshott, M. (1991) *Rationalism in Politics*, Indianapolis, Liberty Fund.

Pulzer, P. (1967) *Political Representation and Elections in Britain*, London, Allen and Unwin.

Qvortrup, M. (2002) *A Comparative Study of Referendums. Government by the People*, Manchester, Manchester University Press.

Ridder, R. (2003) *Campaigning*, Lecture given at Pace University, New York, 18 September.

Rousseau, J.-J. (1913) *The Social Contract*, London, Everyman.

Smith, M.J. (2005) 'Taking part in politics' in Lewis, P.G. (ed.) *Exploring Political Worlds*, Edinburgh, Edinburgh University Press/The Open University.

Verba, S., Nie, N.H. and Kim, J. (1978) *Participation and Political Equality*, Chicago, University of Chicago Press.

Wright, T. (1994) *Citizens and Subjects: An Essay on British Politics*, London, Routledge.

FURTHER READING

Dalton, R.J. (2002) *Citizen Politics: Public Opinion and Political Parites in Advanced Industrial Democracies* (3rd edn), New York, Chatham House.

Denver, D. (2003) *Elections and Voters in Britain*, London, Palgrave Macmillan.

Evans, G. and Norris, P. (eds) (1999) *Critical Elections: British Parties and Voters in Long-Term Perspective*, Sage, London.

Farrell, D.M. (2001) *Electoral Systems: A Comparative Introduction*, London, Palgrave Macmillan.

Norris, P. (1997), *Electoral Change since 1945*, Oxford, Blackwell.

Policy networks and interest representation

Grahame Thompson

chapter 4

Equality & difference

Contents

1	Introduction	106
2	What do we mean by political interests?	108
3	Networks of political power and authority	112
4	Policy networks and the formation of public policy	113
	4.1 Elites	116
	4.2 Corporatism	117
	4.3 Associationalism	118
	4.4 'Associationalism' as a normative idea	119
	4.5 NGOs: networks of dissent	119
5	Multi-level governance	121
	5.1 EU decision making and 'commitology'	121
	5.2 Power sharing and jurisdictions	123
6	Social capital	125
	6.1 Measuring trust	127
7	An evaluation of political networks	129
8	Political networks, state agencies and the market mechanisms	132
9	Conclusion	134
	References	135
	Further reading	136

1   INTRODUCTION

Have you ever 'networked'? ' Networking' has become one of those activities that every self-respecting individual seems to need to do to 'get along' socially, politically and career-wise in the contemporary world. *Who* you know is as important as *what* you know for social success, and networking to establish and reinforce contacts becomes a ubiquitous task for any ambitious person looking to secure success in their social life or career path. But networking in this sense seems to sum up a rather shallow view of how to get on. It can be associated with opportunism and careerism, looking for the main chance rather than caring about the real issues or participating in real debate. For instance, in political terms, it is a substitute for serious political engagement, as a superficial sincerity sweeps across the political spectrum in the wake of the 'spin' and 'deceit' perpetuated by the official political machine.

However, there is a much more serious side to networking. It is one of the main mechanisms by which political power and inequalities are expressed. In addition, it also connects to the way participation and dissent are exercised in political circles. Networks are widespread organizational arrangements through which people express their political interests and aspirations. They have been central to the UK polity, whether in the form of the 'old boy' network, such as that of bankers and other business men (Figure 4.1), or in the form of organizations, such as the Confederation of British Industry (CBI) and Institute of Directors (IoD) lobbying the government on behalf of employer interests. They are part of the way the political process is legitimized. So, networks have become a central aspect of any political system that claims to be democratic (and, indeed, are a feature of almost any form of political system), which raises other important issues about networks discussed later.

There are two related aspects of political networks. The *first* aspect involves the way in which the political system overall has sometimes been considered in terms of a network. Thus, either politics as a whole, though more often certain discrete ways that political policy making and decision taking are organized, can be understood in network terms. This mainly involves four other related ideas:

- either elites or experts actually run politics or account for a major element in political power
- this has more to do with 'associations', so that the field of politics is made up of various private and public associations which act as a definite political formation, and these take on a network character in the way they are linked together

FIGURE 4.1   The British 'old boy' network: bankers meeting

- it can be interpreted as a means by which social interests, or the 'social partners', are mobilized into a structure that actually conducts the business of government and governance somewhat independently of, or parallel to, the main axis of representative politics; and finally

- these are instances of a generic trend in governance terms: the development of what are known as 'policy networks' that directly reconcile different political interest in the formation of public policy making.

For the *second* aspect we need to ask a slightly different question: what are the politics of networks? This involves study of the decision-making nature of network organizational structures with the objective of discovering, for instance:

- whether they are democratic or authoritarian

- how the relationship among various networks is organized politically

- whether they perpetuate or undermine entrenched inequalities of power

- how different groups gain access to networks; and

- whether they are discriminatory devices that are as concerned with excluding some as with involving others.

Clearly these two aspects of the study of networks are closely related, but our purpose is to bring out the two different emphases whenever possible. In addition, we consider these issues in the context of their relationships to the idea of the coordinated governance of a political system. Networks, then, are treated as one of a number of 'vehicles for governance'. The formal constitutional and electoral politics of the UK has been discussed in previous chapters. Here we look at its more informal aspects, those that do not fit neatly into pictures of how UK politics works or is supposed to work but which are, nevertheless, of immense importance.

The underlying theme of this chapter – and an issue that is immediately posed by any talk of networks as political arrangements – is the access different groups or interests might have to such networks. Are they inclusive or exclusive organizational forms? Do they empower some while disenfranchising others? If constitutions and elections grant formal equality to citizens, do informal networks undermine that equality or deepen it? Who has power in networks and who is marginalized by them? The point about these questions is that they raise fundamental concerns about equality and difference. Networks, along with all other forms of political organization, cannot escape these concerns.

Two key concepts will be pursued throughout this chapter: networks and governance. *Networks* are defined as a specific set of relationships making up an interconnected chain or system for a defined set of entities that forms a structure. This is a loose definition, designating little more than a set of interlinked elements that form a coordinating system. Networks are usually thought to operate via the mechanisms of negotiation and bargaining among the elements or players that make up the network. *Governance* encompasses all those processes and interactions that are designed to produce social order in its widest sense, not just the efforts of states or governments. It embraces the relatively standardized practices and institutions that create purposeful outcomes and regulated behaviours in any political system. It is a wider concept than just 'government', which refers to a narrower activity of administrative rule by designated state authorities.

2 WHAT DO WE MEAN BY POLITICAL INTERESTS?

If one of the major roles that networks play in the political system is to give expression to and articulate a variety of interests as they operate politically, we need to define exactly what is meant by the term 'interests'. Interests are characteristics that contribute towards our well-being, or that manifest our outlook relative to others. Such interests can be individual or collective. Individual interests are those advantages that are seen to accrue to a particular person, and which that person might want to protect. Collective interests are interests held by many people in common. In the case of group or collective interests, it could be said, for instance, that it is in the interests of all car drivers that enough road space is provided to allow them to drive their cars relatively freely and safely. One of the ultimate collective political interests is, of course, the 'national interest'. How often have you heard something along the following lines: it is in Britain's vital national interest that it has an efficient and large enough defence force to provide national security against potential military or terrorist threats. In both individual and collective cases, the notion of interests is invoked to indicate something that is part of our well-being or protection, something that contributes to our welfare, to our advantage, or that expresses our values and beliefs. Thus, interests are important for the operation of networks because these mechanisms are one of the main ways people express their interests, either collectively or individually. And they can have a decisive impact on inequalities because, as we will see, access to the right networks can have a major impact on people's life chances and standards of living.

The way interests might arise is dependent upon the way we think that society is organized. The classic case of *group interest* is the Marxist sense of class interests, which argues that the working class has a collective interest determined by its position in the socio-economic hierarchy and that this is completely opposed to the interests of the capitalist class because it is exploited by them. In the past, the era when this conception of interests was most prevalent in the UK was probably immediately after the end of the Second World War when the Attlee Government pursued an overtly socialist political agenda.

Individual interests relates to individuals constructing their self-interests rather more independently of one another, on the basis of the 'rational calculation' of their objectives and constraints. In this case political society is the result of the aggregation of these individual decisions based upon people's own particular interests. Here the era of the Thatcher governments, 1979–90, comes to mind as a period when this conception had its most potent currency.

Were we to adopt a more 'pluralist' approach to social organization, where a plurality of social groups of very different kinds (trade unions, pressure groups, special interest campaigners, householders, individual lobbyists, churches, etc.) constituted society, then the interests of these groups and individuals would arise as a consequence of their 'social locations'. How members of these groups, say, probation officers, road safety campaigners, the Countryside Alliance, moral crusaders, would view the world and its problems would be largely determined by that point of view. But here we encounter a number of issues that impinge upon these particular political inflections of interests. People may have a variety of interests, but how are these interests made politically significant? We will consider three main ways.

First, precisely because there may be a variety of interests, there is a problem of their reconciliation. People occupy different positions in the social hierarchy or milieu, have different outlooks and interests as a consequence, and their interests may be opposed to one another as a result. This may generate conflict among interests. As we shall see, because democracy plays some part in resolving differences as conflicts are elevated to the electoral arena, it falls to the political process to manage such conflicts through the tussle of party politics and the ballot box. Clearly, the issues of power and authority arise in the case of interests, reflecting the inequalities among them, and the fact that there may often be no easy solution to the conflicts they provoke.

Second, how are interests to be made manifest? By what political mechanism are they to be organized? The key category here is that of 'representation'. Interests are represented in the political domain by way of a number of different institutional mechanisms, the most obvious being that of voting. In Chapter 1, Richard Heffernan provided an analysis of the main institutional framework in which voting takes place in the UK – voters elect representatives who represent their constituents' interests in parliament and then form a government. This is the main formal and constitutional framework for a representative democracy. In Chapter 3, Mads Qvortrup showed how different voting arrangements organize the system of representation in any political system. But, as he also showed, there are a number of other ways in which perceived interests might become politically represented, through media publicity, lobbying, public campaigning and demonstrating. With regard to the formation of pressure groups and networks of political action, we need to ask how extensive and effective these are in enhancing 'interest representation'. Of course, the consequence of group formation and activity can reinforce inequalities because some interests are able to secure over-representation, both through the formal electoral process and again through more informal networks.

Third, as social scientists, we need to critically evaluate what is actually happening, to see if democratic representatives can really represent the 'true' interests of their constituents. How do we know whether they have managed to represent the 'true interests' of the people or any particular group? The problem here is that representative democracy always constitutes something that lies between 'true interests' and 'political decisions'. In an indirect, representative democracy it is the representative who speaks and votes for his or her constituents or group members in the decision-making arena, not those constituents or group members themselves. Perhaps something gets lost in this process, particularly if the interests of the representatives are advanced and the true interests of the voters or group members downgraded? Betrayal, compromise and expediency may be rife and are difficult to avoid in any political system (or at least the perception or accusation of such failings is difficult to avoid). Indeed, they are clearly unavoidable if we are not to have a direct democracy, which is too cumbersome for complex decision making in advanced, differentiated and sophisticated polities. The representation of interests certainly still works even here, but it may begin to work via the presentation or making of a *claim* only. Of course, an elected, mandated or assigned decision taker or representative always claims to represent her or his constituents or group members' interests, so we may never quite know what those 'true' interests are, even if they could be properly articulated and aggregated in the first place. If we are dealing, then, with a series of claims to the representation of interests in the political field, rather than 'true' or 'real' interests, where do these claims come from? They must arise *within* the process of political conflict and deliberation itself, not from somewhere 'outside it' or 'before it' in the social milieu or in relation to a deeper set of socio-economic relationships. We do not quite know what group interests actually are until they take part in and engage with the political arena as *political* agents of one kind or another, fighting or making decisions over particular issues.

From this point of view, interests are determined *within* the cut and thrust of actual politics (so they are fluid and dynamic); they cannot be established prior to this and then simply be 'represented' in it. Under these circumstance, networks would be considered as mechanisms that help *shape* interests and inequalities, ones that help establish discriminations and differences. Elections do this as well, of course – help shape the nature of interests – so although the standard analytical framework for understanding UK politics does implicitly assume that interests exist prior to their expression via the ballot box, the point being argued here is a somewhat unorthodox one, and one that goes against the conceptions often shared by both the left and the right of British politics.

Perhaps you can see how this type of a conception might work if we come back to the question of 'the national interest'. Some would say that the 'national interest' is just the interests of this or that class or elite group. They have appropriated the idea of a national interest to suit their narrow purposes. If so, we would be back to a variant of the traditional view outlined above. Increasingly, however, the national interest is something fiercely fought over and claimed. It is difficult to see how it could be just the aggregation of a pre-given set of known individual or collective interests. Politicians are always speaking in the name of the national interest when they are dealing with international political issues, but there are few if any opportunities to establish what that interest is other than by this or that claim to articulate it. Even a referendum on an important international matter that involves issues of the national interest is framed by the limited nature of the question and the prior terms of the political debate about it – precisely a point that would be made by the later critical approach to understanding interests.

SUMMARY

- Political interests can be conceived as individual or collective.
- They have to be 'represented' in decision-making arenas.
- There are a number of mechanisms by which such representation and reconciliation between interests can be organized.
- It may be that interests are only a 'claim' and something that emerges from within the political process itself.

3 NETWORKS OF POLITICAL POWER AND AUTHORITY

The traditional way of thinking about political representation in liberal democratic societies is via the notion of a hierarchical set of layered governmental institutions culminating in the sovereignty of a parliament:

- First, we have local government bodies of various types, each subordinate to some higher authority.

- Second, a set of central government apparatuses, administrative departments of the state, the government itself.

- Third, the sovereignty of a legislature, a parliament, which oversees local and central arrangements.

Governmental institutions themselves are also organized hierarchically, possessing complex relations of subordination and superordination between them, but with the final 'pinnacle of power' situated in a parliament – the sovereignty of parliament. In federal systems of government a more complicated division of power operates, but they share much of the same imagery as outlined here. This downward flow of power is paralleled by an upward flow of representation, so that it is 'the people' that ultimately vest the democratically elected parliament with the legitimacy to rule. In traditional democratic theory, therefore, the key concepts of representation and sovereignty go hand in hand. 'The people' are somehow divided into geographical localities – constituencies – and invested with an 'interest'. These interests are then represented in the relevant legislative arena via the representative they elect for that constituency. Political parties, the instruments of this representational mechanism, mediate between the people, their interests (as suggested in the previous section, all political parties claim to represent an interest), the legislative arena, the government and the sovereignty of parliament.

Against this orthodox conception we can pose a somewhat different approach, a perhaps parallel mechanism that might be thought to capture another aspect to the way governance is organized. In particular, this relates to policy-making and wider decision-making processes, which involve a range of political actors including many from 'civil society' and the marketplace (the 'world of business'). This mobilizes the notions of 'policy networks' involving 'elites', 'corporatism' and 'associationalism'. Policy is increasingly said to be produced by numerous actors negotiating and bargaining one with another, either in pluralist 'policy networks' involving semi-autonomous parliamentary committees and bureaucratic agencies inhabited by experts and specialized policy analysts, or through neo-corporatist consultation ('concertation') between governments and associations representing the interests of business, workers and other societal actors. In addition, in some areas or countries, important aspects of socio-political governance has been delegated to negotiations between 'self-governing' organizations or associations of providers and consumers of collectively financed services.

In the UK, the British Medical Association (BMA) is a good example of this. It deals with the accreditation, regulation and representation of medical doctors and to these ends works with health authorities, trusts and foundation hospitals in which a wider range of interests are involved, among them those of the government, other medical staff, NHS managers and administrators, local governmental bodies and patient groups (see **Charlesworth and Humphreys, 2005**). In addition, there are many networks of dissenting or oppositional groups who claim an authority to campaign on single issues such as the environment, animal rights, and on behalf of 'the poor' and 'disadvantaged'. These latter groups are often collected under the title of 'non-governmental organizations' (NGOs) to indicate their alternative and dissenting character.

For the rest of this chapter we concentrate on how these policy networks operate, in order to illustrate the differences between what might be called various forms of 'networking governance' and traditional notions of 'representative governance', and consider the impacts that these forms of networking governance have on equality and differences in power in the UK and elsewhere.

SUMMARY

- Alongside the formal hierarchical structure of representative government operates a more informal structure of 'network governance'.
- This network governance comprises: policy networks, elites, corporatism, associationalism and dissenting NGOs.

4   POLICY NETWORKS AND THE FORMATION OF PUBLIC POLICY

Two main forms of policy network can be identified: a 'policy community' and an 'issue network' (Jordan and Schubert, 1992; Thatcher, 1998).

A *policy community* is characterized by a largely stable set of interdependent participants, co-existing in a bounded network, who build up a set of shared values and norms and hence form a community that is difficult to break into (the 'insiders' keep out the 'outsiders'). Here, then, is a case where a form of network overtly discriminates and differentiates. Incremental change is typical of this form, where stable interactions and lasting configurations predominate. Policy making is segmented into well-defined subsystems involving a limited and privileged participation. An example of this type of network in the UK is those subsystems involved in education (traditionally including the Department of Education and Science, Local Authorities, the teaching unions, performance review bodies such as OFSTED, schools, academics and education experts). Another example would be agriculture and farming issues, where there has always been a close relationship between the relevant ministry, now the Department for the Environment, Farming and Rural Affairs (DEFRA), the farming community represented by the National Framers Union (NFU), big supplier companies and large customers such as supermarkets. The latter two have been both ferocious in their lobbying and rather successful at it – too successful some would say, the case of genetically modified foods coming immediately to mind.

An *issue network* involves a more open and fragmented network structure, one which is less discriminatory and exclusive. In this case a wide circle of 'policy activists' drawn from a range of interest groups, government personnel, academics and concerned individuals – who are constantly changing – form loosely articulated network groups around specialized ad hoc issues of public concern and policy making. Fundamental change is more possible here, as issues come and go and the make-up of groups alters. Power and dependency relationships are diffused and the locus of decision making difficult to trace. An example of this type of network is the environmental lobbying group, Transport 2000, which is an independent national body in the UK, concerned with sustainable transport (Transport 2000, 2004). It campaigns for less use of cars and more investment in public transport, walking and cycling, arguing that this will reduce the environmental and social impact of transport. One of its many specific campaigns concerns railways. Its rail campaigning and information network, 'Platform', is made up of NGOs, local authorities, rail-user groups, trade unions, community groups and individuals. Another example from the UK, one with a more overtly single-issue focus, would be the case of fuel tax protestors who came to prominence in the late summer and autumn of 2000 (Figure 4.2). This network had a fluid leadership, uncertain membership and an unstable operational base, which soon collapsed when its initial impact had passed.

Policy community and issue network constitute an early classification of policy networks. Subsequently, they found themselves accompanied by a range of alternative claims to describing policy networks (Jordan and Schubert, 1992; Rhodes and Marsh, 1992; Thatcher, 1998). This was in part a response to the perceived weakness of the policy community/issue network duality. This distinction covered only part of the policy-making process. In particular, it ignored agenda-setting aspects, the original distribution of power among the potential participants, technological and economic factors that impact upon the formation and operation of networks, the macro-institutional context in which various networks exist, and an explicit address to questions of change (Atkinson and Coleman, 1992). Other approaches brought in many of these

FIGURE 4.2   The fuel crisis in the UK: lorry drivers protesting

issues by adding a wider set of contextualizing features and political agents into the policy-making structure, in particular, questions of overall form of the state and the potential for macro-interest group mediation. These are discussed later.

However, why should the general issue of policy networks, and this increasing range of claims to describe them, have become such a significant element in political analysis? In part, this has to do with a set of changes in the way societies were perceived to operate. Among the possible features here are:

- the emergence of the *organized society*, or society based on organized collectivities

- a trend in most reasonably sophisticated political systems of *sectorization* in policy making

- the increased mobilization of competing interests which leads to *overcrowded policy making*

- the increased *scope of state policy making* – perhaps as a result of the electoral 'auction' which forces political parties to appear to offer solutions to everything

- the *decentralization* or the *fragmentation of the state*. There are few state goals but an aggregation of departmental interests

- the *blurring of boundaries* between public and private. Policy making tends to be made between factions of the state and clientelistic interest groups.

(Jordan and Schubert, 1992, p.11)

In this context the whole policy-making process becomes a more fragmented and relatively open system made up of competing interests vying for their voice to be heard and their influence to be felt. These systems involve complex and sometimes unstable combinations of competition and coordination, negotiation and the exercise of power, independence and interdependency, and consultation and the exercise of pressure politics. Even within governments, interdepartmental coordination between semi-autonomous lower level units is increasingly designed to be solved through bilateral or multilateral negotiations among the participants, rather than through the hierarchical direction of chief executives (in the manner of so called 'joined-up government' in the UK). In addition, public service provision often depends on inter-organizational cooperation within networks of formally autonomous or de facto independent semi-public and private sector organizations.

Thus there is a range of approaches to understanding the nature of these policy-making structures. But for the rest of this section we concentrate on just four mentioned in the previous sections: elites, corporatism, associationalism and dissenting NGOs. Although these are generic terms, each encompassing a number of variants, they are different enough from each other to give a flavour of the overall range of characterizations.

4.1 Elites

Elite groups involve those with particular access to power and influence. Such groups may be constituted by wealth or status, often inherited. Alternatively, they may be class based, sharing a common political and cultural outlook. In liberal democratic societies these are sometimes known as 'the establishment' or in the specific UK context of the public school and Oxbridge 'old boy network', linking men (and less often women) of high finance and industrial muscle with politicians and those in top administrative positions in the government or Civil Service. One such example of an elite group, then, would be top business people, a kind of 'financial-industrial oligarchy', whose activity is to manage much of the economic resources of a country. Economic clout, personal ties and a shared cultural outlook means they wield a great deal of power, perhaps unaccountable power. In addition, in as much as they share convictions and similar outlooks with political elites, they can influence – some would say unduly influence – political processes as well.

'Elite' networks are, therefore, different from 'democratic' policy networks in that they can be based upon birth or inherited wealth and influence. And it is the role of elites in the informal governance and coordination of power that explicitly raises the problem of the lack of accountability of that power within important areas of social life. Elites can serve to circumvent the proper conduct of democratic politics, particularly those associated with electoral outcomes, by organizing influence behind the scenes, bringing their own interests to bear upon decisions. They involve a select and small-scale group, held together by reciprocal bonds of loyalty and trust. But elites are genuine 'non-egalitarian' networks. They are marked out by birth or status, which also gives them a decidedly hierarchical feel. They are one of the mechanisms by which power inequalities can be reinforced, differences reconfirmed and reproduced. In fact, elites are not well integrated into an analytical framework that looks explicitly at policy networks, precisely because they seem to hark back to an older era of political organization, one where power and influence were the direct result of birth or wealth rather than of 'negotiated interests'. And this is exactly what is being challenged in corporatist theories of government.

4.2 Corporatism

Corporatism is a political theory stressing the way large interest groups, the 'social partners' as they are sometimes referred to, combine semi-informally in a cooperative manner to regulate and govern central aspects of social life. Thus we might see the government bargaining with the organizations of large and small industrialists, with agricultural interests, with the financial sector, and with organized labour, or some other important social groups such as consumers or environmentalists, to establish a modus vivendi on an important social, political or economic issue. In these arenas, cooperation is generated by means of bargaining and negotiation between formally specified and recognized actors. But this procedure means that parties must resist unilateral actions and must observe mutual obligations otherwise the network will degenerate. In principle, therefore, these networks are more inclusive than the elite networks, though they serve to do much the same thing.

Some analysts have seen whole countries partly or largely governed along these lines, where the social partners or interest groups are integrated into an established regulatory order that can dampen potential conflicts among them before they break out into a more open conflict. In this way a consensus can be built up informally and, as a result, the business of government can be conducted in a more conciliatory manner. Once again, however, this process tends to bypass the normal channels of political lobbying and representation. It operates as a kind of macro-scale network in the conduct of governing a polity. The period when this type of framework was thought to be most active in the UK was during the 1960s when Harold Wilson was Prime Minister. It involved the National Plan, the National Economic Development Office, the Industrial Reorganization Corporation, and 'beer and sandwiches' meetings in Downing Street involving the government, the unions and (less often) employers' groups.

The status of corporatism in the current period, however, is unclear. Some see it as a failed and outmoded form of governance, something that typified the inflexible and rigid systems of economic management operating during the 1960s and 1970s, which were largely swept away by the neo-liberal turn in policy matters of the 1980s. Margaret Thatcher, for instance, was particularly keen to rid the UK of the lingering corporatist influences of the Wilson years when she formed her first government in 1979. However, whether these macro-corporatist arrangements did actually wholly disappear in the 1990s remains controversial. Some have argued that they survived, re-inventing themselves as part of a turn towards 'social compacts' designed to protect vulnerable sections of the population otherwise subject to the increasing insecurities and uncertainties associated with 'globalization' (Hirst and Thompson, 1999; Crouch *et al.*, 2001). Since the mid 1990s there may therefore have been a revival of this form of economic neo-corporatism, bringing with it macro-network type of governance, though one found most prominently in the smaller or more economically vulnerable states of western Europe.

4.3   Associationalism

The third form of these alternative political conceptions considered here is associationalism. This represents a more pluralistic version of corporatism (see Streeck and Schmitter, 1986; Hollingsworth, Schmitter and Streek, 1994). This particular approach stresses a wider range of political associations in which people invest their political allegiances, energies and 'sovereignt*ies*'. Where elites and corporatism could be argued to re-empower the already powerful, reinforcing inegalitarianism, associationalism is thought to be more inclusive and egalitarian. It challenges the idea that there is a single dimension to sovereignty, as organized along hierarchical lines. Instead, it stresses the dispersal of sovereignty, and with it the representative mechanism that supports it, suggesting that sovereignty is (or should be) dispersed throughout a series of 'political' organizations to which any individual might owe an allegiance. These organizations govern the range of private interests existing in any society. There is thus a plurality of sites where the sovereignty of the people rests, some of which may not even be considered political in the usual sense. These could include places of employment, professional societies, trusts, commissions, churches and even companies. On a somewhat larger scale, this idea has been promoted as a model for a particular kind of 'negotiated state'. This involves the articulation of voluntary self-governing associations into a macro structure of power, what Paul Hirst has termed 'associative democracy' (Hirst, 1994). But it should not be forgotten that the origin of much of the discussion of associationalism is grounded in a specifically UK discussion among guild socialists and political pluralists in 1920s and 1930s Britain, particularly the work of Harold Laski, G.D.H. Cole and J.N. Figgis.

4.4 'Associationalism' as a normative idea

This model of 'associational democracy' emerged from the shadow of a claim about how societies *are actually* organized politically to become one arguing how they *should be* organized politically. It makes a normative claim to say how things could be better organized to suit a more democratic and plural objective, to create a more egalitarian and effective democratic political order. Within this model, semi-autonomous, democratically organized associations, each conducting its business on behalf of its members, would rely upon state financial subsidies and would be conditioned in what they can do by state law. Each of these associations would be constrained to provide a certain level of service to its members as a condition for the receipt of state finance, but members would be able to leave and join other associations if they so wished. This system is not, however, directly hierarchically organized or coordinated. Policy choices are not pre-empted by the unilateral prerogative of a hierarchical authority, but are shaped by the constellations of preferences negotiated among the associated network members.

Thus there are two separate ideas of 'associationalism' at work here. On the one hand we have the idea of associationalism as akin to the private interest governance of Schmitter and Streeck, which is meant to be a *description* of things as they are already found in the political arena. They make one of the claims to say how existing policy networks are actually formulated and organized. 'Associational democracy', on the other hand, is an aspirational and normative suggestion as to how political decisional making could, and indeed *should*, be organized so as to overcome what are argued to be inadequacies and inequities of contemporary social governance. Thus, here we have an example of the difference between a positivist analytical description of the political process and a normative suggestion as to how it might be improved.

4.5 NGOs: networks of dissent

A somewhat different deployment of the idea of networks operating in the political field involves the role of non governmental organisations (NGOs) in network governance. These appear as something of a counterweight to the essentially 'participatory communities' just described. NGO networks provide the 'other' of the elite and establishment influence on governance, although in some ways they are a variant of the notion of 'associationalism' considered in Section 4.3. NGOs are essentially private interest associations, but ones concerned with campaigning and propaganda for a particular purpose. Examples include Greenpeace, Oxfam, Amnesty International, Help the Aged and Save the Children (Figure 4.3). Their objective is to change public policy (either to persuade governments to do something or to stop doing something), usually by mobilizing public opinion and putting pressure on the established policy frameworks from the outside. Thus NGO networks speak directly to the

"I'm desperate for a cause."

FIGURE 4.3   The 'other' of network governance

problems of power, inequality and difference. They are seen as 'bottom-up' organizations, speaking directly for the disadvantaged and forgotten.

But NGO activity is always faced with a real dilemma. Should these organizations stay 'outside' the political mainstream and remain part of a pressure politics, or should they cooperate and become part of the more formal policy network environment? Of course, the issues and dilemmas that are brought out here and which face NGOs in an acute manner, are problems and issues that are faced by all types of networks, which are discussed further in Section 7 below.

SUMMARY

- Policy networks can be of two basic kinds: policy community and issue network.

- Policy networks arise because of the progressive fragmentation of the political framework for decision taking.

- Elites are a form of network based upon privilege and exclusion.

- Corporatism is a macro-network structure of inclusion based on the conciliatory decision making of the social partners.

- Associationalism involves coordination and governance by widespread associations of private interests.

- Dissenting NGOs represent networks of 'outside' pressure, but are always faced with the dilemma of inclusion as the means to real influence.

5   MULTI-LEVEL GOVERNANCE

In recent years a conception that is different from, but related to, that of policy-making networks has entered the discussion of political governance. This is the notion of 'multi-level governance'. Multi-level governance refers to the particular problem of coordinating the activities of layered dimensions of governance. In a macro-context this can involve relations between local, regional, national, supranational and transnational bodies (Hooghe and Marks, 2001). In the absence of overarching political mechanisms that establish a hegemonic or hierarchical imposition on the political order, it requires the skills of negotiation and bargaining among parties situated at the different levels in a familiar pattern to that just discussed in the case of policy networks.

These kinds of administrative arrangements are thought to strongly typify certain aspects of European Union (EU) decision making. On the one hand, *horizontal* policy coordination at the local, regional, national, transnational and supranational levels is conducted through bilateral and multilateral negotiation on issues such as environmental pollution, economic integration and communication regulation. On the other hand, *vertical* policy coordination requires a similar pattern of behaviour but now organizing relationships *between* these administrative levels.

5.1   EU decision making and 'commitology'

The mechanisms for making decisions in this multi-level governance framework can be classified as 'joint decision systems', 'expert committees', and 'open methods of coordination' (OMC). These have been further summed up under the term 'commitology', which indicates the central role that committees of experts increasingly play in EU decision-making procedures in particular (and in which the UK now takes a prominent part).

Commitology refers to the systems of specialist expert committees appointed by member states that advise the European Commission and prepare regulatory proposals for a vast range of EU activity. They operate by consensus, through self-reflective deliberative debate, comparison and benchmarking across the different EU member states, establishing rules and technical specifications. These specifications most often provide a framework within which the member states compare and elaborate their own final regulations. They do not so much harmonize rules across Europe, but rather provide a forum for joint deliberation and the space for the operation of 'national treatments'.

The OMC structure has more to do with procedures for integration and is associated with economic development and social inclusion. It involves public–private partnerships, NGOs, relevant statutory authorities and local social partners. They operate through iterative, critical comparisons of local initiatives, moving between the European Commission and national implementation plans in a cycle of consultation, strategy making, guideline establishment, implementation monitoring and surveillance, and the reassessment of priorities. The classic example of this is the European Employment Strategy, but an important precursor was the process of developing the euro as an EU common currency, which involved the now famous Delors Committee. In June 1988 the European Council, which comprises the Heads of Government of EU members plus their Foreign Ministers, decided to set up a committee under the chairmanship of the President of the European Commission, Jacques Delors. The committee was composed of heads of the 13 members' central banks (acting in their personal capacities as experts), plus three other noted authorities on monetary matters. Its terms of reference were 'to study and propose concrete stages leading towards economic and monetary union in Europe'. The members provided a series of papers to the committee, which drafted a short final report that was submitted to the European Council the following year, known as The 'Delors Report' (Office for Official Publications of the European Communities, 1989; Figure 4.4). The rest, as they say, is history.

FIGURE 4.4   Jacques Delors and members of the European Council, Madrid, 1989

What this demonstrates, then, is the important role such committees, based upon a network of experts, can play in the formulation of EU policy. This is sometimes termed an 'epistemic network', a policy community based upon some common and shared knowledge (in this case, the nature of banking and monetary policy), inhabited by experts who broadly agree on technical and practical matters. In addition, however, the success of this committee in establishing the key agenda for EU economic integration was the skilful political preparation, manoeuvre and lobbying of its chairman, Jacques Delors. He acted as the key 'policy entrepreneur' in securing political support during the committee's deliberations, making its presentation to a wider policy audience and, crucially, in then steering its proposals through the multi-levels of the EU governance hierarchy.

5.2 Power sharing and jurisdictions

One key element in the concept of multi-level governance is the *allocation of authority mechanisms* between its different levels: either under a principle such as that of subsidiarity in the case of the EU (that decisions should be left to the most appropriate level where their legitimacy and effectiveness is greatest); or the dispersal of policy-making powers in the case of decentralization or devolution in other contexts, such as in the case of the UK. Both trajectories involve the reconfiguration of existing jurisdictions and the creation of new ones, with authority capacities being reformulated accordingly.

This kind of power sharing across multiple jurisdictions is often thought to be more efficient in grounding policy decisions in an environment that elicits credible commitments from the parties involved. It is argued that such power sharing can better reflect the heterogeneity of preferences and interests of different constituencies situated at the different levels. The monopoly appropriation of decision-making authority by central state bodies looks vulnerable to these competing interests and constituencies. Multiple jurisdictions also allow for some jurisdictional competition, which can be good for governance and regulatory innovation.

Hooghe and Marks (2001) suggest there are two types of multi-level governance.

- The *semi-federalist option* or one that lends itself easily to intergovernmental relations or complex local to national level coordination. This option conceives of the dispersion of authority to a limited set of non-overlapping jurisdictions at a limited number of levels. These jurisdictions bundle authority into quite large packages, and they are relatively stable.

- The *polycentric option,* with overlapping geographical territories and functional domains, pictures governance as a complex, fluid patchwork of innumerable overlapping jurisdictions. These jurisdictions are lean and flexible, coming and going as demands change, and their competencies are also highly fungible. The whole idea is for this framework to be flexible and to respond to changing citizen expectations and preferences, and to be sensitive to functional requirements as they evolve.

Thus, these two images parallel policy communities and issue networks, the two forms of policy networks considered in Section 4. It is the second of these types that most easily lends itself to be envisaged in typical networking terms. The first type would seem to operate more formally. In addition, as the example of the Delors Committee process showed, the semi-federalist form demonstrates the way networks can reinforce hierarchical governance, consolidating existing inequities in the access to power and influence. The Delors process, which involved only a tiny elite of monetary and banking experts – mainly the European Central Bank Governors or Presidents – was certainly not open or democratic, although the subsequent implementation process was subject to the usual political checks and balances that operate in the EU.

But how can we conceptualize the actual way decision making is organized in these kinds of networks? Two overall approaches can be discerned, which themselves rather depend upon how the operation of networks as such are themselves conceived.

First, we have a conception that says networks are fundamentally no different from any other institutional mechanism in how their internal business is conducted, even though they might include an extended range of participants. Networks involve differences of power and authority in terms of those agents and participants that are members, so it all amounts to the deployment of these power or authority capacities. In this case policy networks are little different in their effects from other more traditional forms of political representation. They operate the same inclusion/exclusion mechanisms, keeping power close to those in the network and deliberately marginalizing those excluded from it, jealously guarding the privileges of a limited network access. All the usual modes of bargaining and negotiation can come into operation here; the deployment of guile and cunning, not declaring one's total hand, the operation of rhetorical and persuasive skills, and the ability and talent in making alliances. No outcome can be quite predicted in advance, despite the fact that some will have an obvious superior advantage over others, and can use their greater power to their own ends.

Second, there is a conception that networks are somewhat different institutional mechanisms, ones that operate according to an altogether different decision-making logic. Here, it is claimed, networks are typified by rather 'flatter' organizational structures where power is evenly distributed so that all parties have a more equal chance of their views being listened to and taken into account. These institutions rely upon cooperation and consent, not just the operation of power politics in a different environment. They are typified by the attributes of trust, loyalty, honesty, solidarity and cooperation in the articulation of their decision making capacities. In this case, negotiation and bargaining take on a different form: the seeking out of a genuine cooperative, consensual and coordinated outcome to which parties will voluntarily commit. Under these circumstances the issue is how one can understand the formation of this process where different and often conflicting 'private' interests are originally involved. In general this kind of a conception would stress the attempt of policy networks to be more inclusive, to welcome a more active citizenry and be open to marginalized groups and voices. They would also stress the importance of bargaining and negotiation in network situations. Bargaining describes situations of interdependence where interaction takes place under the assumption that the players can come to a binding agreement about sharing the total gains.

SUMMARY

- Multi-level governance is a form of networking that addresses the problem of coordinating decisions across different levels and dimensions of governmental activity.
- 'Commitology' is a particular decision-making structure – favoured in the EU – that relies upon expert committees to develop and monitor policy.
- There are two forms of multi-level governance: semi-federalist and polycentric.
- There are two ways in which networks are conceived to work internally: via the usual deployment of power and authority; or via a more conciliatory, deliberative and consensual approach.

6   SOCIAL CAPITAL

The importance afforded to trust in network situations associated with political decision making and the effective operation of politics more generally is demonstrated by the discussion of 'social capital'.

Social capital expresses the degree of citizen involvement in community affairs, which, it is argued, powerfully influences the performance of government and social institutions (Coleman, 1998; Putnam, 2002). It is a category explicitly associated with 'social inclusion', so it emphasizes the way differences and marginalization might, if left unattended, undermine social cohesion. In recent years it has been taken up by such organizations as the UK government, the World Bank and the Organization of Economic Cooperation and Development (OECD), which have tended to use it as another way of encouraging 'community values'. Like everything else in politics it seems, social capital is a disputed category and has a number of definitions. Most of these include some notion of the way networks combine with shared norms and understandings to facilitate cooperation within or among groups.

As the argument goes, civic traditions, like local networking – in which agreed norms of behaviour and trust among participants are encouraged – generate social connectedness and social participation, enabling participants to act together more effectively in the pursuit of shared objectives. Put simply, the more people are connected to one another, the more they trust one another and the more this serves civic ends.

The UK government in particular has become interested in social capital, which it sees as a natural complement to its emphasis on inclusion, social engagement and economic performance. The Performance and Innovation Unit (a body attached to the Cabinet Office) draws a distinction between three types of social capital:

- *bonding* social capital – characterized by strong bonds (or 'social glue') e.g. among family members or among members of an ethnic group;

- *bridging* social capital – characterized by weaker, less dense but more cross-cutting ties ('social oil') e.g. between business associates, acquaintances, friends from different ethnic groups, friends of friends;

- *linking* social capital – characterized by connections between those with different levels of power or social status, e.g. links between the political elite and the general public or between individuals from different classes.

(Aldridge *et al.*, 2002, pp.11–12)

Clearly, there is a simple logic at play here, which many have found a compelling one. In one of its most celebrated formulations, Frances Fukuyama (1995) finds in social capital's underlying logic the key to the *cultural* determinants of the whole of social progress and economic prosperity. He argues against the idea of a purely 'economic' explanation for prosperity. Instead, he foregrounds the social virtues of trust and association as a better basis for making and sustaining wealth, prosperity and economic competitiveness. For Fukuyama, the political implications of social capital are of equal if not greater importance than the economic progress made possible by the combination of rational economic action and traditional virtues of civic action. Spontaneous sociability and a healthy capitalist economy go together; sufficient social capital in the underlying society permits businesses, corporations, networks and the like to self-organize, throwing off the mantles of authoritarianism and state intervention. In turn, these conditions are the hallmark for a healthy capitalist economy.

In dealing with social capital, Putnam (2002) analysed the effectiveness of regional governance in Italy, where there was a thoroughgoing reform in the 1970s, which established strong regional governments. In some regions, mainly in the north, he found social and political networks were organized horizontally, not hierarchically. These 'civic communities' valued solidarity, civic participation and integrity. Here, democracy works. On the other hand, there were the 'uncivic regions', mainly in the south, where a pervasive atmosphere of authoritarianism still prevailed. Trapped in these interlocking vicious circles, nearly everyone feels powerless, exploited and unhappy. Here, unsurprisingly, representative government is less effective than in the more civic communities.

6.1 Measuring trust

The main means for assessing the level of trust in societies comes from surveys of social attitudes such as the World Values Survey (WVS) or the British Social Attitudes Survey (BSAS). These measure trust as the willingness of the average citizen to trust others, including members of their own families, fellow citizens, people in general and institutions of various kinds. The UK Cabinet Office uses the BSAS survey to assess the level of trust and social capital in the UK and Table 4.1 shows how trust among people varied across regions in the UK in the late 1990s.

TABLE 4.1   The level of social trust by region, Great Britain, 1998

Region/country	Respondents[1] (%)
South east	50.3
Scotland	50.3
South west	47.0
Wales	44.9
North west	44.0
East Anglia	42.9
Yorks and Humber	41.9
East Midlands	40.8
West Midlands	40.0
North	38.2
Greater London	36.6
Great Britain	**43.9**

[1] Percentage responding, 'Most people can be trusted', to the question, 'Generally speaking would you say that most people can be trusted or that you can't be too careful dealing with other people?'
Source: adapted from Aldridge et al., 2002, Table 4, p.19

Perhaps of equal interest, the European Commission regularly asks people how much they trust political institutions, and this varies significantly across countries as shown in Table 4.2 (overleaf).

TABLE 4.2   Average level of trust in political institutions

Country	Level of trust[1] (%)
Luxembourg	58
Denmark	54
The Netherlands	52
Sweden	49
Austria	47
Ireland	44
Finland	43
Spain	40
Portugal	40
Belgium	40
Average for EU15	**36**
Germany	35
Greece	34
United Kingdom	34
France	30
Italy	29

[1] The average level of trust in four institutions as a percentage by country. The four political institutions asked about were: the civil service, the national parliament, the national government and political parties.
Source: *Eurobarometer No.57*, Full Report March to May 2002, p.7

The result for Italy shown in Table 4.2 is interesting, particularly in light of Putnam's discussion of Italy mentioned above. Clearly, there may be some differences between north and south Italy, but Italians as a whole seem highly distrustful of their national political institutions. The result for the UK is equally striking, and could be disturbing.

One issue thrown up by the existence and effects of social capital is the question of how it is fostered and created. For Putnam, social capital in the Italian regions was the direct result of civic traditions originating in the nineteenth century. In the case of the USA he also stressed the contribution older civic traditions had made to US social capital, which he considered to be now under threat (Putnam, 2000). For him, social capital is a precarious commodity, deeply embedded in the history of societies – once undermined or spent, it is very difficult to recreate.

Some commentators have questioned Putnam's concerns about the destruction and long-term decline of social capital, suggesting that changes might instead be a sign of its *transformation*. Direct, informal social engagement may be giving way to new indirect and more abstract forms. If so, then 'bonding social capital' might be giving way to 'bridging social capital', to adopt the terminology cited above. Here, developments such as cheaper travel and internet access could be possible instruments for this transformation, alongside recent emphasis on legal redress, rights charters and performance indicators, all of which could provide a more individualized citizenry with the means to civic engagement under radically changed social and cultural circumstances. To which could be added, as we shall see, various public policy initiatives to encourage 'linking social capital'.

SUMMARY

- Social capital is thought to be an important attribute of networks, facilitating democratic policy making and civic participation.

- Trust is seen as a key ingredient of social capital.

- Levels of trust vary considerably across regions and countries.

- There is a lively debate about whether trust and social capital are declining or being transformed.

7 AN EVALUATION OF POLITICAL NETWORKS

We have explored a number of alternative, but connected approaches to the understanding of political organization, contrasting them with an 'orthodox' position. Each of these approaches displays some of the features of a network structure. Each of them also gives us some insight into the actual way politics works. Clearly, they do not exhaust the insights because the orthodox representational case continues to have much to offer. Each complements the other, running very much in parallel to each other, highlighting particular aspects of a complex whole.

We have seen that networks partly shape and form inequalities and differences in society. A first point, then, is to ask whether these networks are essentially undemocratic? Clearly they do not totally conform to traditional notions of 'representative democracy'. As we have seen, elites, for instance, may become cliques, groups or bodies of partial and unrepresentative interests who can exercise great power and influence and exclude other forms of networks access to these. In addition, that power and influence is unaccountable in any obvious democratic fashion. Networks of business personnel founded on interlocking corporate directorates, for example, may weld together men and women of high finance and industrial muscle who can decide matters informally among themselves. Those decisions then have a profound impact on the economy and beyond. But how can any collective influence be effective if the power so controlled is neither visible nor accountable? Indeed, how can elected representatives properly conduct their own legitimate business if they face similar obstacles? The British 'old boy network' may act to usurp and undermine genuine democratic government. If you happen to be in a network, that may work to your advantage, but if you are one of those left out you may just have to put up with it.

A second and related set of criticisms of networks focuses upon the 'informal rationality' that pervades these types of coordinating mechanisms. This is contrasted with the 'procedural rationality' that is thought to typify both hierarchical and market forms of governance and coordination. The advantage of procedural rationality is that it tends to be open, explicit and rule driven. It is either bureaucratic or contractual. Thus, it is not so obviously open to possible manipulation and abuse as an informal rationality might be. Informal rationality relies much more upon the operation of discretion. It allows the agents in the network to make decisions according to what suits their purpose and whim. The fact that the network relies more on discretion leads to the awkward problem of potential corruption. Who is to monitor and police informal networks? Of course, corruption and abuse are not immune from the market or hierarchy either, far from it. But there would seem to be more scope, in principle, for this to arise if discretion becomes the dominant characteristic of network operation. For instance, in some ways the Mafia is the perfect network structure: it relies upon trust, loyalty and solidarity (but not honesty!), and would seem to operate with a wide scope for pragmatic discretion.

In fact we might take this assessment of networks even further. It has been suggested that the attributes of a robust, cohesive and long-term policy network are found in the notions of trust, loyalty, honesty and the like, but one could point to policy networks where just the opposite characteristics were present. Some networks might work on the basis of fear and suspicion. In particular, this can be the case if groups of otherwise competing 'insiders' are faced with an even greater threat from a group of 'outsiders'. Here, the insiders can generate some form of alliance in the form of a network, to try to deal with the threatening outsiders and defend themselves against that threat. Despite the mutual suspicions among them, it is the insiders' greater fear of the outsiders that leads them to establish and sustain a working network among themselves. Something along these lines led to the formation and sustaining of many lobbying networks of British firms when faced with the threat from foreign, particularly Japanese, competitive suppliers in the 1970s and 1980s.

Finally, it may be that policy networks are now being eclipsed by new forms of policy making that have drawn the whole process further into either the framework of hierarchical organization or more into the ambit of market power. There are two indications of moves in this direction.

The first is exemplified by the emergence of what in the UK are called quangos (quasi-governmental organizations). These organizations, which have been imposed upon the policy-making process from above, arose as the public domain was compartmentalized into a myriad of agencies, boards and trusts in conjunction with the imposition of quasi-privatized quality standards, audits and managerial direction resulting from the 'reform' of the public sector (Skelcher, 1998). These boards, trusts and agencies 'compete' with one another in terms of meeting their targets for service provision as they are ordered into hierarchical league tables of ex-post performance. The result is an odd combination of competition and command, where the ultimate authority has increasingly been appropriated into a command (or hierarchical) style of operation.

The second involves the development of policy units staffed with special advisors attached to departments of government; they provide 'private advice' on policy matters directly to government ministers. This bypasses both traditional policy networks and the traditional advice and responsibility of permanent Civil Servants. The rate of turnover of policy initiatives, one following rapidly after another, seems to have increased in the UK, and is partly fuelled by these developments. But this is aided by the appearance of an additional layer of policy making, that of 'think tanks'. The proliferation of these organizations, all trying to win the ear of government, has stimulated an entrepreneurial culture of policy making and led to a quickening of the pace of policy turnover.

All these developments reconcentrate policy-making power centrally. The creation of policy units, the quasi-governmental boards, trusts and agencies, and the operation of think tanks are not democratically organized and the personnel who are appointed to them are not elected or subject to the usual terms of accountability (Figure 4.5). For instance, Skelcher (1998) estimated there were 70,000 *appointments* to UK quangos by the late 1990s. They have become the fiefdoms of politicians and the government in particular. In many ways these new arrangements undermine the more widely dispersed sub-agency 'policy networks' where a larger range of interests were involved in policy making and decisions. They can certainly serve to keep NGOs well away from the centre of political decision making.

SUMMARY

- It is questionable whether policy networks are democratic in the way they operate.

- Networks are not necessarily open and participatory, they can be closed and based upon fear.

- The emergence of 'managerialism', quangos, agencies, think-tanks and the like may be recasting the policy-making landscape, and recentralizing it.

FIGURE 4.5 The alternative way of policy making: centralized and unaccountable

8 POLITICAL NETWORKS, STATE AGENCIES AND THE MARKET MECHANISMS

The changing context in which public policy-making and decision-making networks exist is indicative of the relationships that exist among policy networks, governmental agencies and the market system in general. Clearly, policy networks have always operated in the shadow of the market, majoritarian rule or hierarchical authority – something which may have enhanced the effectiveness of networks and other governance modes and the outcomes emerging from their interactions. In this sense, then, networks have proved effective governance mechanisms that complement other forms of governance. This idea that networks have operated in the 'shadow of hierarchy' relies upon the ability of a hierarchical authority to affect lower level interactions without coordinating these directly or unilaterally. It builds upon a distinction between a *hierarchical authority structure* (something difficult to avoid in matters of governance) and *hierarchical direction* operating to override decision preferences of other actors (Scharpf, 1997). The former rests upon a threat, while the latter rests upon an intervention. Clearly, where there are networks of self-organization and self-government existing in the shadow of the state, we have a case of a hierarchical authority structure, but one where the state does not directly coordinate decisions and the activity of the networks in any great detail. Instead, the state establishes the rules under which networks operate. Policy networks can, therefore, be seen as agencies that *enhance* the effectiveness of traditional hierarchical governance, rather than operating as an alternative to it that might undermine it. Of course, 'negotiating states' or 'neo-corporatism' are an example of more overt direction, where the state intervenes to establish collective outcomes by negotiating as a party with the other associations or social partners, or acts as an 'honest broker' to bring these together under its auspices. This is sometimes expressed as 'private-interest governance' where the state enforces compulsory membership and shepherds the parties into negotiations. Again, however, a form of hierarchy is reinforced by this mechanism.

Yet, in as much as the above analysis has stressed the self-organizing and self-governing characteristics of policy networks, one would expect these networks to resist being steered by the state and to jealously guard their own autonomously generated decision-making environments. So, adopting a highly managerialist perspective on overall network governance could be seen as undermining the rationale of networks, and this remains a real threat. On the other hand, a more managerial stance might actually enhance the long-term viability of networks by providing the conditions for a sensible extension or support for their autonomy, and thereby preventing network closure or fracture. One of the great problems with networks is that they can become inward looking and defensive, as mentioned above, so there need to be some mechanisms to monitor and prevent this.

However, returning to the consequences of the 'vertical' shadow of the state, the UK presents a classic case of the relationships operating here. This does not so much involve the hesitant moves towards devolution in the UK case, although it involves this in some part (see Chapter 2), but has more to do with the fragmentation of the direct policy-making process. The UK has been one of the main centres for the development of the 'policy network' approach to coordination and governance, but this may now have been overtaken by subsequent events that have often been summed up under the broad term of 'managerialism'. As mentioned earlier, the UK has seen the proliferation of quangos as various semi-private/semi-public partnerships, boards, trusts and agencies have been charged with policy-making and policy implementation activities, organized around performance targeting and quality control procedures. This regime has now been joined by a growing number of 'policy units' attached to government departments, thus attaching another layer to the overall policy-making process. Combined with the proliferation of think-tanks closely connected to governments, we can see an attempt to take the process closer to a conventional hierarchical model. It may be, then, that UK policy networks in the traditional sense are being squeezed by a newly reinvigorated hierarchical trend. The *shadow of hierarchy* is growing and intensifying in the form of closer administrative attention from the state apparatuses of Whitehall. Certainly, Whitehall does not seem to want to be caught out without a policy as unexpected events unfold.

That said, policy networks are, of course, also squeezed from a different angle, from the *shadow of the market*. From this point of view, managerialism is a somewhat contradictory process. It involves not only a strengthening of hierarchical control but also involves introducing a number of market-inspired innovations that bolster it. Competition among agencies, the development of public–private partnerships and more accurate pricing of public services are the modalities of this particular part of the process. In the UK, for instance, the state-run National Health Service remains little more than a large 'command economy' where resources are allocated centrally, and most prices set centrally, but where its 'branches' – hospitals, health surgeries, trusts and boards – 'compete' with one another to provide the actual output, under the guidance of benchmarked norms, targets and quality indicators. This looks suspiciously like a form of 'market socialism', but, whatever else it is, it does not look very much like a traditional network structure.

SUMMARY

- Official policy networks work in the shadow of both the state and the market.
- Hierarchical authority impinges on networks in various ways.
- There may be renewed pressure from hierarchical authority that is recentralizing the policy-making process and undermining the operation of policy networks.
- Policy networks also operate in the shadow of the market as well as the state, and this too threatens to transform traditional policy networks.

9 CONCLUSION

This chapter has taken a broad-brush look at the way the concept of network has been appropriated into the realm of political analysis and political policy making. The key concept of a 'policy network' has been used as a general term to designate a wide range of different forms of political coordination and governance. The debate about the appropriateness of these different designations, be they elites, associations, corporatisms or NGOs, provides the opportunity to examine the way the notion of a network is invoked as an organizing principle. Naturally, politics and economics are closely linked in the formation and understanding of policy networks. The idea of 'social capital' offered a clear example of this linkage, tied up closely as it is to the context of comparative economic performance.

The overall conclusion of the chapter, however, must be that policy networks are under severe pressure, caught in a pincer movement between an increasingly confident shadow of hierarchy and an equally strident shadow of the market. Indeed, whilst one might say that policy networks have always been placed under a shadow of hierarchy – and rightly so since they need this as a regulatory condition and to maintain the necessary 'openness' to their operations – the contemporary turn in their activities is to re-appropriate this business into the traditional mainstream of policy making *within* government in a much more forceful way than has been experienced in recent decades. More and more of the policy-making process seems to be being brought back 'in-house'.

Of course, the market also hovers over this in two ways. First, more and more of the traditional public sector business has been directly privatized or semi-privatized. Second, the remaining public sector activity has itself been subject to the dictates of a market-inspired regime of internal scrutiny and performance assessment. These twin moves, then, may be heralding the demise of the policy network paradigm, or significant aspects of it, not only in the UK, but also throughout Europe and the USA where similar pressures and moves have been felt over recent years. These moves do not seem designed to directly tackle entrenched powers of inequality and difference. Rather, they seem designed to bury both, in either the bureaucratic morass of indicators and quality assurance norms or the economic incentives driven by market norms. Certainly, then, as we have seen, there is much more to political networks than just 'networking'.

REFERENCES

Aldridge, S., Halpern, D. and Fitzpatrick, S. (2002) *Social Capital: A Discussion Paper*, Performance and Innovation Unit, The Cabinet Office, April.

Atkinson, M.M. and Coleman, W.D. (1992) 'Policy networks, policy communities and the problem of governance', *Governance*, vol.5, no.2, pp.154–80.

Charlesworth, J. and Humphreys, W.D. (2005) 'Challenging centre–periphery relations in health policy' in Prokhovnik, R. (ed.) *Making Policy, Shaping Lives*, Edinburgh, Edinburgh University Press/The Open University.

Coleman, J.S. (1998) 'Social capital in the creation of human capital', *American Journal of Sociology*, vol.94, S95–119.

Crouch, C., LeGalès, P., Trigilia, C. and Voelzkow, H. (eds) (2001) *Local Production Systems in Europe: Rise or Demise?*, Oxford, Oxford University Press.

Fukuyama, F. (1995) *Trust: The Social Virtues and the Creation of Prosperity*, London, Penguin Books.

Hirst, P.Q. (1994) *Associative Democracy: New Forms of Economic and Social Governance*, Cambridge, Polity Press.

Hirst, P.Q and Thompson, G.F. (1999) *Globalization in Question*, Cambridge, Polity Press.

Hollingsworth, J.R., Schmitter, P.C. and Streek, W. (eds) (1994) *Governing Capitalist Economies: Performance and Control of Economic Sectors*, New York, Oxford University Press.

Hooghe, L. and Marks, G. (2001) *Multi-level Governance and European Integration*, Boulder, Rowman and Littlefield.

Jordon, G. and Schubert, K. (1992) 'A preliminary ordering of policy network labels', *European Journal of Political Research*, vol.21, nos.1–2, pp.7–28.

Office for Official Publications of the European Communities (1989) *Report on Economic and Monetary Union in the European Community*, Luxembourg, EU.

Putnam, R.D. (2000) *Bowling Alone: The Collapse and Revival of American Community*, New York, Simon & Schuster.

Putnam, R.D. (ed.) (2002) *Democracies in Flux: The Evolution of Social Capital in Contemporary Society*, Oxford, Oxford University Press.

Rhodes, R.W.A. and Marsh, D. (1992) 'New directions in the study of policy networks', *European Journal of Political Research*, vol.21, nos.1–2, pp.181–205.

Scharpf, F. (1997) *Games Real Actors Play: Actor-Centric Institutionalism in Policy Research*, Boulder, Westview Press.

Skelcher, C. (1998) *The Appointed State: Quasi-Governmental Organizations and Democracy*, Buckingham, Open University Press.

Streeck, W. and Schmitter, P.C. (eds) (1985) *Private Interest Governance: Beyond Market and State*, London, Sage.

Thatcher, M. (1998) 'The development of policy network analyses: from modest origins to overarching frameworks', *Journal of Theoretical Politics*, vol.10, no.4, pp.389–416.

Transport 2000 (2004) 'Moving forward on transport', www.transport2000.org.uk/ (accessed 3 August 2004).

FURTHER READING

Hooghe, L. and Marks, G. (2001) *Multi-level Governance and European Integration*, Boulder, Rowman and Littlefield.

Marsh, D. and Rhodes, R.W.A. (eds) (1992) *Policy Networks in British Government*, Oxford, Clarendon Press.

Putnam, R.D. (ed.) (2002) *Democracies in Flux: The Evolution of Social Capital in Contemporary Society*, Oxford, Oxford University Press.

Thatcher, M. (1998) 'The development of policy network analyses: from modest origins to overarching frameworks', *Journal of Theoretical Politics*, vol.10, no.4, pp.389–416.

Analysing politics: constitutional reform

Jeremy Mitchell

Contents

1	Introduction: rules, constitutions and constitutional change	138
2	Constitutional change and political argument	141
	2.1 'Underlying principles' arguments	143
	2.2 'Pragmatic' arguments	143
	2.3 'System design' arguments	144
	2.4 Constitutional reform and the political parties	145
3	Recent constitutional change in the UK	147
	3.1 Positions of the parties	147
	3.2 Constitutional principles and conventions	148
4	The problem of the House of Lords	154
5	A brief history of Lords reform	157
6	Conclusion	162
	References	165
	Further reading	166

1 INTRODUCTION: RULES, CONSTITUTIONS AND CONSTITUTIONAL CHANGE

I recently joined a club and received a membership card with a set of the club rules. These outlined the structure of the organization that I had joined, listed its objectives and the benefits of membership. It set out the organizational structure that exists to achieve the club's objectives: the roles of the chair, treasurer, secretary and club committee; the number of members on the committee; how long the office holders and committee members serve, and their role in the day-to-day management of the club. There were details about its general financial structure too – the subscription fees and the methods of accountability that exist. The function of the annual meeting of members was described, together with the various reports that are made at this meeting by the office holders. The rules also outlined the mechanisms through which the members can replace the committee or can change decisions made by the committee between the annual meetings. Finally, it specified how the rules themselves could be altered.

This will all be very familiar to people belonging to similar organizations – local societies, trade unions or other groups such as the National Trust. You will recognize that the membership rules of the organization also define the institutions and office holders, the mechanisms and processes through which the organization operates, and the general framework within which its activities take place. However, the rules are subject to interpretation and there may well be differences between the functions and activities described by the rules and the actual way in which the organization runs. There is often a gap between the 'ideal' – as set out in the rules of any organization – and the 'reality' of its day-to-day operation. Informal institutions and processes may be as important as those set out in the formal rules. Action can be taken, and policy made, by members acting together outside formal meetings. Such networks of individuals can be essential for the functioning of any organization. Institutional culture is important, too. Although nowhere explicitly stated it may, for example, be assumed that this year's secretary becomes next year's president, and this will have consequences for how the club runs. In a similar way to some of the policy networks described by Grahame Thompson in Chapter 4, 'elites' can establish themselves in clubs as well as in society at large.

For much of the time *how* the club operates will not be in question, provided the organization fulfils its declared purposes and keeps its members happy. But if the satisfaction of the club members does decline, then the members have a number of options. In Hirschman's phrase they can exercise 'exit, voice or loyalty' (Hirschman, 1970). So, disaffected members can leave the club, exercising their 'exit' option, to find an alternative organization that may produce more satisfactory benefits for them. A second option is that they can try to mobilize other members to 'voice' their concerns collectively, and so change either the club policies or its office holders, or both. The third option is to do nothing, remain loyal, and hope that things get better. There is a parallel here with 'real' politics. In both cases there may be differences of opinion, policy is often contentious and disagreements may only be resolved through an appeal to the membership or the wider electorate.

When such disagreements are extreme, provoking deep or irreconcilable differences, then the club may need to change how it operates and alter its rules; it may need to change its constitution. To do this, it may have to consult the membership, and perhaps hold an extraordinary general meeting to discuss and agree any fundamental changes. The club rules will say how this can be done. It may be straightforward, requiring approval by only a majority of members, but often the rules state that such a major change has to follow a special consultation procedure and requires the approval of more than a simple majority of members, perhaps a special majority of those at an extraordinary meeting or some other minimum quorum of the members.

There are obvious parallels between the functioning of such a club and of many wider political systems. Both are organized for a specific purpose. Both have defined institutions for 'the governance of persons and the administration of things': office holders in the case of a club, political institutions in the broader political system of a nation-state. In both settings the institutions define a structure of opportunities and set out potential rewards for individuals and groups. In both cases 'the rules of the game' may be set out formally; in the rules for the club and in the form of a constitution for the nation-state.

In a similar manner to the club rules, therefore, 'constitutions are codes of rules which aspire to regulate the allocation of functions, powers and duties among the various agencies and officers of government, and define the relationships between these and the public' (Finer, 1979, p.15). In most political systems these are codified in a document – known as a constitution – that has a special status in relation to other laws. This operates in two ways. First, it is often difficult to amend a constitution and it may require special procedures to do so. Second, and as importantly, in any conflict between 'ordinary' legislation and the provisions of the constitution, it is the constitution that prevails and the legislative action that is nullified. An independent supreme court, as in the USA, usually makes rulings on conflicts or potential conflicts (see Chapter 1).

Just as a club may need to adapt and change in response to external events, the same can be true for political systems too. In 1958 Algeria was still ruled by France. The French state was faced with violence from an Algerian independence movement, together with unrest among the French settlers in Algeria, over the government response. The problems were exacerbated by the possible political intervention by the armed forces in French politics. The failure of the political institutions in this crisis was one major contributory factor behind the change from the Fourth Republic to the Fifth Republic (Figure 5.1). This involved the adoption of a new constitution, and with this a redefined set of political institutions.

FIGURE 5.1   France, 1958: (left) crowds of anti-Gaullist demonstrators marching in Paris and (right) General Charles de Gaulle at a press conference on becoming president of the French Fifth Republic

Such a total or fundamental change is relatively uncommon in democratic political systems. Most constitutional change is evolutionary and partial. In France the change was introduced through a referendum and the new constitution, and the political regime it would usher in, was approved by a majority of the political community and enjoyed broad popular support. But even when there is no direct popular consultation, for constitutional change there are often special provisions for changing the political rules. So Article V of the US constitution provides that any proposed reform should be supported either by a two-thirds majority of both houses of Congress, or 'on the Application of the Legislatures of two thirds of the several States, shall call a Convention for proposing Amendments, which ... shall be valid ... as Part of this Constitution, when ratified by the Legislatures of three fourths of the several states ... '.

These provisions make it relatively difficult to amend the US constitution and help to ensure that a proposed change has extensive support within the political community. However, as Richard Heffernan stressed in Chapter 1, both the constitution and the process of constitutional change are very different in the UK. As he suggests, the political system of the UK has three key features:

- a flexible, easily amended constitution
- a unitary state
- a parliamentary democracy.

The Westminster system is a majoritarian one in which the central executive – the government – usually has extensive, although not unlimited, powers through its control of a party majority in the House of Commons. There is a further difference between the UK system and many other political systems, such as that of the USA, that have a codified constitution. In the UK, constitutional legislation is no different from other legislation; there are no special provisions for its enactment. This has important consequences. Because constitutional legislation is no different from ordinary legislation, arguments about constitutional change may be similar to arguments about other policy differences, and the evidence used to support or challenge any proposals for change may be similar too.

SUMMARY

- Political systems are organizations with rules defined within a constitution.
- Such constitutions are often codified documents and in any conflict between the constitution and other legislative action it is the constitution that prevails.
- To be altered or amended, many constitutions require special provisions.
- The constitution of the UK is not codified and does not require special provisions for change.

2 CONSTITUTIONAL CHANGE AND POLITICAL ARGUMENT

To consider the possible relationship between evidence and argument over constitutional change let us go back to the organization that I joined and see what happened when a financial crisis threatened its continuing existence. The club developed a growing financial deficit and it needed to increase its regular income. There were only two ways it could do this. It could either increase its annual membership dues – and hope to maintain its current level of membership – or it could broaden its membership base and so generate more income at the same level of membership fees. Both courses of action required a change in the club rules. In both cases, too, there was a clear link between the arguments advanced, the need for a rule change and a possible increase in the overall club income, and a 'solution' to the problem that the organization faced.

Is this also true about arguments over constitutional change in the UK? Let us look at the case of the proposed changes to the composition of the unelected House of Lords, the 'Upper House of Parliament', the second chamber of the legislature. At the time of writing it is composed of some hereditary peers, able to sit for their lifetime but no longer able to pass their membership to their male children, together with life peers, archbishops and bishops of the established Anglican church, and high court judges. The Lords (Figure 5.2) has certain legislative power to revise proposals presented to it from the 'Lower House of Parliament', the elected House of Commons, but in the event of a disagreement between Lords and Commons, the Commons can – in most cases – prevail.

FIGURE 5.2   The House of Lords in session debating the hunting bill

The future form of the House of Lords has been the subject of much debate, particularly since 1997 when the Labour Party was elected with a programme of reform. Since the Parliament Act of 1911 the power and authority of the unelected Lords has ebbed considerably, particularly as the power of the elected Commons has increased. Accordingly, as Richard Heffernan outlines in Chapter 1, the UK legislature has shifted from a relatively symmetrical bicameralism (having two legislative chambers, each chamber having equal power) to an asymmetrical bicameralism (where one of the two chambers has more power than the other). Before 1958 all members of the House of Lords, known as peers, were hereditary; that is, their title and right to sit as a member of parliament was passed on through the generations, in most cases through the male line, but the passage of the Life Peers Act 1958 saw the introduction of life peers, nominated by the prime minister, who sat as peers only for their lifetime. The Labour government came to office in 1997 determined to abolish the membership of hereditary peerage in the second chamber, which it partially did in 1999. Stage one of Lords reform, removing most hereditary peers, has been achieved, although a parliamentary deal saw 92 of them permitted to remain members for the time being; stage two, further reform of the chamber (now that the hereditary element is being phased out) has, however, been the subject of considerable disagreement.

Are, then, arguments about the reform of the House of Lords similar to those about solving the financial crisis of my club? Is there a clear link between the reforms proposed and the 'problem' of the House of Lords either in terms of its composition or its powers? The answer is no. And this is not just because there is no clear and agreed outcome for constitutional change over reform of the Lords. There are, however, certain parallels. Arguments about constitutional change are also 'constructed' arguments that advocate a particular reform and select particular supporting evidence. Most arguments about constitutional change fall into one of three categories – each of which draws on a different kind of evidence.

2.1 'Underlying principles' arguments

The first type of argument is based on, and appeals to, some underlying principle, such as democracy, equality or utility. In proposing changes to the House of Lords this type of argument stresses the unrepresentative composition and undemocratic nature of the present chamber and suggests, as a matter of principle, that it is not appropriate for a non-elected body to play a significant legislative role in a democracy. Supporters of this type of argument point out that for a legislature to be democratic and legitimate, to enjoy the support of the political community, it should be composed of representatives who in turn reflect the wishes of that wider political community. Citizen preferences are expressed through voting in free and fair elections, so the principles that apply to the election of MPs and to other levels of this political system, should also be extended to play a role in determining the composition of the House of Lords. Additionally, arguments based on 'democratic principles' might also note the problems inherent in the extent of prime ministerial patronage, which still plays a major role in determining the membership of the House of Lords through the creation of new life peers.

2.2 'Pragmatic' arguments

A second type of argument avoids theory or abstraction; it does not draw on underlying principles, but argues from the concrete, from the 'facts' and 'realities' of particular communities and traditions to suggest that what is best is what 'works'. Those who advance this type of argument suggest that you do not need abstract principles to describe British politics or political institutions. So, in the case of the House of Lords, a supporter of the status quo or of minimal change would suggest that although the current second chamber is not perfect, it works and is useful, perhaps even essential, for the functioning of British government. They might argue, too, that starting from scratch, one would not necessarily produce the current house either in terms of composition or of powers, but because the House of Lords is the result of a series of political compromises over time, it is a solution to specifically British political problems and conditions. Such an argument might also stress the gradual nature of much political change in the UK and suggest that institutions need only adapt to changing conditions, not embrace radical or revolutionary change. We should note that the first and second types of arguments also differ in the nature of the evidence to which they appeal – the first emphasizing abstract ideas and principles, the second embracing more empirical concerns.

2.3 'System design' arguments

Like the first, a third type of argument accepts the case for reform but links changes in the representative role of the second chamber to larger questions of institutional design. Reform of any one element of the political system cannot, and should not, be considered in isolation from the workings of the system as a whole. Supporters of this type of argument would note that all bicameral systems tend to have a different form of representation for each of their two houses. Particularly in federal systems, one chamber is often based on the election of representatives by popular vote, the other on geographical representation. In the UK, only the House of Commons is elected and the government is – usually – formed by the party able to command majority support in the Commons. In other political systems the second chamber may be elected too, but in a different way. It could, for example, be based on equal representation by area irrespective of population. In Germany the upper house, the Bundesrat, is composed of delegations from each state or *lander*. In the USA, each of the 50 states has two of the 100 representatives in the Senate, whatever its population or electorate. So Rhode Island, the smallest US state, has the same number of senators as California, the largest. The other US legislative chamber, the House of Representatives, is composed of 435 members of congress elected for similar-sized districts, so that Rhode Island has only one representative, but California has 53. With regard to House of Lords reform, then, this type of argument suggests that it may be appropriate to reconsider the basis of its composition and how it should or could be differentiated from the Commons. Finally, if you do have two legislative chambers and they have a different composition, then you cannot assume that a majority government in one chamber will also have a majority in the other chamber. So you need to consider how to resolve differences between the two chambers – although there might be some advantages in establishing the composition and relative powers of the two chambers before considering how such differences could be resolved.

This third type of argument considers reform within the context of the wider political system, and so would note that recent constitutional changes have established devolved institutions in the nations and regions of the UK – a Scottish Parliament and Assemblies in Wales and Northern Ireland (as Montserrat Guibernau discusses in Chapter 2). These do not have full legislative powers equal to those of the Westminster Parliament but their creation has changed the unitary nature of the UK state. Perhaps changes to the Westminster parliament should recognize this through a change to the representational base of a revised second chamber and give it a more specific role in representing the regions of the UK. Such arguments might also suggest that part of the current impasse over the reform of the House of Lords may derive from the piecemeal changes of the past, from a failure to consider wider institutional design.

2.4 Constitutional reform and the political parties

The three types of argument share certain characteristics: all select and use particular evidence. In the UK, political argument is usually advanced by and through political parties and each of these three types of argument can be associated with a different one of the three major British political parties.

First, the Labour Party, is still, in theory at least, committed to a more democratic and representative second chamber. Its manifesto for the 1997 general election committed it to reforming the House of Lords by removing its hereditary element, but there was no agreement over future reform. The party leadership currently advocates a wholly appointed second chamber, other Labour MPs support some degree of election, often with an element of appointment as well. Partly as a result of the government's commitment to appointment, the Conservative Party now largely favours a predominantly elected second chamber. For them the elected element should represent the regions of the UK and would be elected on a different basis and to a different electoral timetable from the House of Commons. This represents a change to their previous position. Until recently the Conservative Party saw the House of Lords as in little need of radical change and their policy was based on arguments of the second type.

If the first type of argument emphasizes the role of abstract principles and underlying ideas, and the second stresses the evolutionary nature of British politics, then arguments about institutional design involve the use of comparative evidence, how other political systems operate – and how this might be relevant in a UK context. For the Liberal Democrats the increasing devolution of powers to the nations and regions of the UK should be accompanied by the reform of the House of Lords to create a second chamber representing these nations and regions – as in federal systems such as those of Germany and Australia. Some reformers go further and suggest that it is time to replace the uncodified constitution of the UK with a codified one written down in a single document. As in the case of the club rules with which we started, this would specify the nature and purpose of institutions, the relationships between them and how they might in future be changed through constitutional reform.

If political arguments draw on particular evidence then two other points are important. First, as in the case of the reform of the House of Lords, the political parties may advance different types of argument. In doing so, they draw on different types of evidence and as a result they may 'talk past each other' rather than engage in an exchange that can be resolved by any appeal to a common body of evidence. For example, those arguing from democratic principles talk about voting and equality, while more pragmatic traditionalists talk about 'what works'. But, second, arguments about constitutional change may become part of the more general policy debate among parties. So, in 1997 the Labour Party was in favour of a reformed House of Lords probably with some elected element; now the Labour government favours a wholly appointed house. The Conservative Party used to support heredity and appointment; now, with most hereditary peers having been ousted, it sees a role for elections. To some extent this reflects the wider policy competition between the parties, but the debate is more complex as there are differences within parties as well as between them. For instance, some in the Labour Party wish to see a predominantly or even wholly elected House of Lords. As a result, there may be implicit or even explicit alliances among members of different parties on this particular issue, particularly if the House of Commons is given a free vote (a vote where the party does not tell its MPs how they should vote). This is different from the normal policy disagreements among parties. To understand why this occurs, and how the nature of the argument has changed, we need to look both at constitutional arguments in general, and at the particular case of Lords reform.

SUMMARY

- Arguments about British constitutional change are normally offered from three different, broad perspectives: those based on democratic ideas (underlying principles); those referring to the gradual and evolutionary nature of political change in the UK (pragmatic); and those stressing the questions of institutional design (system design).

- These arguments tend to be supported by different types of evidence.

- Because they draw on different bodies of evidence the different arguments may 'talk past' each other.

- Partly because of this, and as constitutional change does not require special legislation in the UK, debate about change may become part of the more general policy debate among parties.

3 RECENT CONSTITUTIONAL CHANGE IN THE UK

To try to understand recent constitutional change in the UK, and the problems of political reform, we need to look at some of the major recent proposals, the attitudes of the major parties and at the constitution itself.

3.1 Positions of the parties

The perceptions of constitutional change found in the policies put forward by the political parties are important. These perceptions have an impact on what different individuals think is 'evidence' for change (or continuity). That, in turn, affects the nature of the arguments offered. These perceptions are rooted in party histories and experiences.

In the 1970s the Labour government under Harold Wilson became increasingly concerned about the growing electoral success of the Scottish National Party (SNP) and Plaid Cymru (PC) in Scotland and Wales respectively. In both countries this success seemed to be at the expense of the Labour Party. Labour was heavily dependent on winning seats in Scotland and Wales in order to win a majority of seats at Westminster. So the loss of support to the nationalist parties could undermine its ability to form a UK government.

One contributory factor to the rise of Scottish and Welsh nationalism was the perceived remoteness of the Westminster government and its lack of responsiveness to local concerns in the constituent nations of the UK. So, the Wilson and Callaghan governments proposed a change in the structure of political institutions with some powers devolved from Westminster to elected assemblies in Scotland and Wales. These more local institutions would be better able to respond to local, regional and sub-national needs and concerns – and so could reduce the electoral appeal of the nationalists. This was presented as an argument of the first type (ideas based) – the changes would produce greater democratic responsiveness and accountability. At the same time, the devolved assemblies would still exist within the overall UK framework under the centralized authority of the Westminster parliament.

The proposals were controversial and were opposed not only by the Conservative opposition but also by some within the governing Labour Party. The arguments within the Labour Party were complex. One strand in the discussion emphasized that any change in institutional arrangements might make a future Labour government less able to enact general policy at Westminster. Some policy making would now be the responsibility of the devolved institutions and Labour representation at Westminster could also be reduced – this was an argument of the second type (reality based). According to the Conservative opposition, the proposed changes would undermine the essential unity of the UK; as one politician put it 'there is no half-way house between government by Westminster and an independent Scotland and Wales' (Powell, 1978). Because Labour opponents ensured that the Scottish and Welsh referendums to introduce devolution had to secure the support of 40 per cent of the total electorate, not just a majority of those who turned out to vote, the proposal was rejected as it drew insufficient support in both nations. When the Scottish and Welsh Nationalists withdrew their support for the minority Labour government, this in turn contributed to the government's defeat in a Commons vote of confidence in March 1979, prompting a general election which the Conservatives won. Not until 20 years later, after the election of 1997, when wider support existed in the Labour Party in both Scotland and Wales, was the change finally put into effect and devolved institutions established (as Montserrat Guibernau notes in Chapter 2).

In terms of Lords reform, there has been an even longer delay between the passing of the Parliament Act of 1911, which reduced the power of the House of Lords to block parliamentary legislation passed by the Commons, and the further reform of the functions and powers of the second chamber in the British parliament. Almost a century later, although the 1911 Act was regarded as a temporary measure when it was passed, reform of the Lords is still not completed. If, as Richard Heffernan suggests in Chapter 1, the executive is largely in control of the legislative timetable – which it is – and if constitutional legislation does not require any special provision – which it does not – then, as illustrated by Lords reform, why is constitutional reform so difficult to achieve in the UK?

Some partial answers come from considering two overlapping questions: the nature of the UK constitution, and the reasons why changes to it are proposed. So we need to examine the nature of constitutional arguments to see how change is achieved and how constitutional disagreements are resolved.

3.2 Constitutional principles and conventions

The UK constitution is based on several sources, some written, some not. Crucially, unlike the constitutions of the USA or France, the UK constitution does not exist as a single written text; it is uncodified. Part of it does derive from parliamentary legislation, but where this is the case, the amendment of constitutional legislation is no different from the amendment of other legislation. It therefore requires no special majority. However, as the constitution derives from several sources, there is not necessarily one pattern to constitutional change. The major sources of the constitution are set out in Box 5.1.

BOX 5.1   **Finding the UK constitution**

Statute law   Acts passed by parliament that can be amended by parliament; for example, the successive Representation of the People Acts which have defined and redefined the possession of basic political rights, such as the right to vote. Often changes to such basic rights, as in the lowering of the voting age to eighteen, enjoy all party support. This may imply the existence of a broad consensus for such changes, so that they can be enacted quickly and will be widely accepted. This is not always the case – the Conservative Party did not support the establishment of devolved institutions for Scotland and Wales in 1997–99.

Common law   Law unaffected by statute law and mostly derived from rulings by the judiciary in areas where parliament has not legislated. Some rights, such as freedom of speech or of assembly, are not positively guaranteed – as they are in the US constitution – but exist as it were by default where they are not limited by other existing legislation. The position on many basic rights in the UK was strengthened with the incorporation of the European Convention on Human Rights (ECHR) into UK law.

European Union law   Such law ultimately derives from the various treaties agreed among the member states of the EU. These now determine how the government can, and cannot, act in some policy areas, including trade, agriculture, environmental and employment policy. In these areas European law may override UK law.

Royal prerogative powers   These include the right of the prime minister to head the government, to appoint and dismiss ministers, to allocate and reallocate portfolios, to appoint peers and senior bishops, to confer honours and, most significantly, to sign treaties and declare war. These were formerly part of the role and power of the monarch but most of the royal prerogative powers have now passed to the executive, in effect to the prime minister.

Constitutional conventions   There are a number of assumptions that shape political action to which all members of the political community adhere. For example, it is by convention that the prime minister can now only sit in the House of Commons, or that after a general election the leader of the largest party in the Commons will be asked to form a government. Conventions are not legally defined and frequently derive from unarticulated common assumptions. They are also historically formed and subject to evolution. The interpretation of a convention may change over time and any convention is only effective as long as everyone accepts and acts by it. Some conventions are, however, explicitly formulated. After 1945, the Labour government had some of its legislation rejected by the House of Lords, but the government eventually reached an agreement with Lord Salisbury, then the leader of the Conservative Party in the House of Lords. The 'Salisbury convention' means that the House of Lords will not oppose government measures that derive from a manifesto commitment, and so have received popular endorsement.

Authoritative constitutional commentary   Some of these have come to have constitutional implications. One the most important of these is *Erskine May's Treatise on the Law, Privileges, Proceedings, and Usage of Parliament* (May, 1997; first published 1844). It has been revised frequently since then and provides precedents or guidance on the process of legislating and how the House of Commons should work. Such commentaries may influence how legislation is enacted and as a result have constitutional implications.

The variety of these elements has several consequences. Unlike many other political systems there is no mechanism to signal that an ordinary law is in conflict with some constitutional principle. So statutory provisions may override non-statutory ones, later statutory provisions will replace earlier ones, and so on. The constitution is constantly changing in other ways, too, as conventions are discarded and modified, or different interpretations are put on existing ones. However, the sovereignty of parliament is the central fact of the British political system and the main source of constitutional change through legislation.

With no special provision for constitutional legislation, reform in the UK could, in theory, be both frequent and straightforward. Indeed, as Box 5.2 demonstrates, the Labour government has brought in several constitutional changes since 1997.

This period of constitutional activity is in marked contrast to the preceding period, which saw little constitutional change. Perhaps the only major measures passed between 1945 and 1997 were the abolition of the university seats and double member constituencies in 1947; enacting the Parliament Act of 1949, which further restricted the powers of the House of Lords; introducing life peers in 1958 and allowing peers to renounce their titles in 1963; lowering the voting age to eighteen in 1970; imposing direct rule from Westminster on Northern Ireland in 1972; and joining the European Economic Community (as the EU was then called) in 1973. What lies behind this pattern of reform activity? Why has reform been difficult or slow historically and why has this changed recently?

Consider the various reforms in Box 5.2. They derive from several different sources. Some were a manifesto promise of the incoming Labour government – such as the establishment of devolved institutions in Scotland, Wales and Northern Ireland, and the incorporation of the ECHR into UK law. In the case of the Scottish Parliament and the National Assembly for Wales, the commitment dates back to the previous Labour government of 1974–79 (Figure 5.3). The Conservatives did not support this reform, but electoral success in the 1997 general election gave the new Labour government a mandate to introduce such change. Other reforms, such as altering the electoral system for European elections and signing the Amsterdam and Nice Treaties, came from external, European commitments, and would eventually have been enacted by any government.

BOX 5.2 **Some major constitutional initiatives since 1997**

The Human Rights Act 1998 introduced the European Convention on Human Rights into British Law.

After regional referendums some legislative powers have been devolved to new institutions in Scotland, Wales and Northern Ireland and a directly elected London Mayor and Assembly has been established. Other municipalities have been given the right to opt for local mayors as well.

The Government agreed to the EU Amsterdam Treaty in 1998 and the Nice Treaty in 2001.

Since 1999 elections to the European Parliament have been held under a closed list system of proportional representation.

In 1999 most hereditary peers were removed from the House of Lords, the Wakeham Commission was established to chart further reform of the second chamber, a task later given to a Lords–Commons Joint Commission. Stage 1 reform complete, the removal of most hereditary peers, no agreement has been reached on the form that Stage 2 reform will take.

A Freedom of Information Act, albeit one with limited power, was enacted in 1999.

The Electoral Commission was established in 2000 to register political parties, to oversee a new transparent regime for the finances of political parties, to control election spending, and oversee and review the conduct of elections and referendums.

FIGURE 5.3 The result of recent constitutional changes: (left) the Scottish Parliament and (right) the National Assembly for Wales, in session

There was much disagreement and debate about these proposed changes. The evidence used by the political parties to support their arguments – and disagreement usually followed party lines – reflected the distinctions introduced earlier. We can see this in the example of the incorporation of the ECHR into UK law and the accession to the Amsterdam and Nice Treaties. All were opposed by the Conservative Party. For them the Amsterdam Treaty signalled a further transfer of sovereignty and power from Westminster to the EU, and the incorporation of the ECHR involved a diminution of the autonomy of the British government in areas of individual rights. For Labour, on the other hand, the incorporation of the ECHR marked a further extension of basic democratic rights. Here, again, we see a contrast between an approach that stresses underlying (democratic) principles, and one that takes a more 'pragmatic' line.

Partisan disagreement is not always present. As society changes it may be necessary to adjust the institutions of government to reflect these changes. Consider the example of the problems associated with party funding and the financing of politics that emerged towards the end of the Conservative government in 1997. In this case the establishment of an independent Electoral Commission to monitor political finance had broad, all party, support. However, in general the two major parties do have different attitudes to constitutional change. The Labour Party is often in favour of government action as a way of transforming political institutions or adjusting perceived inequities (and thus associated with 'principles-based' reform); the Conservative Party is more reluctant to consider purposive intervention and tends to avoid radical change of the constitution (therefore associated with 'pragmatic-based' reform). Conservatives might also note the unintended or negative consequences of some changes and prefer to rely more on the slow adaptation of existing institutions.

While there is often disagreement over the end results of proposed constitutional change, part of the problem may also derive from the lack of an agreed process for making such changes. If constitutional legislation is no different from ordinary legislation then it can be introduced by any administration with a working majority in Parliament. But any such change could then be reversed after a change of government. To avoid continuing instability and uncertainty there has been an assumption that constitutional reform should enjoy bipartisan or all party support. This is frequently difficult to achieve and, as a consequence, constitutional reform can be slow. If the parties disagree about the extent and role of government – which they do – then change in the political institutions that play an important role in the process of governing can be particularly difficult to achieve.

On the issues that most directly affect the nature and power of central political institutions – the reform of the structure of parliament, changes to the electoral system that determines the composition of the House of Commons and the devolution of power to subordinate authorities in the nations and regions of the UK – there does tend to be sharp disagreement both between political parties and sometimes within them too. In these cases the issues and proposed solutions are often highly contentious, and reform may be slow and tortuous as a result. This is certainly the case in the history of parliamentary reform, particularly reform of the House of Lords. The Labour government elected in 1997 had a large parliamentary majority; it could claim a popular mandate for reform, as many of its constitutional measures had been foreshadowed in the party election manifesto. In some areas it was able to enact reform legislation relatively easily, in cases where such reform involved the creation of new institutions rather than the adaptation or change of existing ones.

However, this was not true for the reform of the House of Lords, a part of parliament that can also play an active role in the legislation that is being enacted for its own reform. Here the arguments reflected the different attitudes of the major parties that were discussed earlier. For Labour, reform of the House of Lords was a further extension of democracy, the completion of a process of institutional change that had been begun almost a century earlier. For the Conservatives, the proposed changes were partisan constitutional engineering, the unnecessary adaptation of an effective and functioning institution. For the Liberal Democrats the reform of the second chamber provided an opportunity to adjust the overall structure of parliament and political institutions (reflecting the 'institutional design' rationale mentioned earlier). While they had a different preferred institutional outcome, the Liberal Democrats agreed with the Labour government that this was an opportunity to modernize UK political institutions.

If the basic arguments used by the three parties differ, then the type of evidence they use to support their arguments differs too. So perhaps it is not surprising that it is difficult to reach an agreed conclusion. The recent history of Lords reform provides a case study of institutional change in the UK that clearly illustrates the relationship between political argument and political action.

SUMMARY

- The uncodified UK constitution has several elements: statute law, common law, EU law, royal prerogatives, constitutional conventions, authoritative constitutional commentary. As a consequence there is no single mechanism or process for changing the constitution.

- While some constitutional initiatives are relatively straightforward, agreed reform of existing institutions may be a long drawn-out process, as is demonstrated by reform of the House of Lords.

- The arguments used to support constitutional change may draw on very different types of evidence, marshalled for very different purposes.

4 THE PROBLEM OF THE HOUSE OF LORDS

A study by Tsebelis and Money found that about only one in three of the world's polities are bicameral with the passage of legislation involving two distinct chambers (Tsebelis and Money, 1997). In the UK, the House of Commons and the House of Lords have broadly the same legislative competence. With the exception of money bills, legislation can be introduced in either house and becomes law when it has passed both houses in identical form, and has received royal assent. However, the two chambers do not have equal powers. The Lords can amend legislation that comes to it from the Commons but such amendments can usually be overridden and the wishes of the Commons can prevail. This is not always the case, and the Lords can delay legislation by making amendments that, owing to lack of time or the pressure of events, the Commons might accept in order to expedite final passage. In exceptional circumstances, should the Lords insist on opposing a bill or reinserting its amendments, then the House of Commons may lose the bill at that parliamentary session. However, under the Parliament Act, the Commons is able to override Lords objections the following year by passing the same bill unamended by the Lords.

The House of Commons is the popularly elected 'democratic' chamber, whereas the House of Lords has no popular mandate. In this case is it 'right' that the second chamber can frustrate the wishes of the 'democratically' elected House of Commons? If this occurred with any great frequency it could make government more difficult, if not impossible. So what should be done? Does the problem lie in the powers of the second chamber, what it can or cannot do, or its constitution and composition, the fact that it is unelected and lacks popular legitimacy? Should its functions (Box 5.3) or its membership – or some combination of the two – be changed? And how should reform be proposed? On the grounds of utility, the practicalities of the legislative process and the requirements of effective government? Or by ideas about democracy, institutional design and constitutional theory? Or perhaps partisan party policy?

There are major differences between the Lords and Commons in terms of their composition, political complexion and relationship to the government. Most importantly the Commons are elected, but the Lords are not. In late 2003 the Lords was composed of 92 residual hereditary peers and 579 appointed peers. The composition of the Commons changes after elections; normally one party has a majority and forms the government. But the Lords is not dissolved at the end of a parliament. Until 1999 the main element of the second chamber was the hereditary peerage, so its composition changed only as hereditary peers

> **BOX 5.3**   **The contemporary functions of the House of Lords**
>
> The House of Lords:
>
> - provides a forum for debate on matters of public concern
> - initiates legislation including government bills and private members bills
> - scrutinizes the activities of the executive
> - has a set of select committees that examine areas of public policy.
>
> However, its status as a 'second' chamber also implies that some important measures, such as money bills, originate in the House of Commons and that it may:
>
> - revise public bills brought from the Commons
> - consider delegated legislation (where the government is given broad powers by a bill, but a minister decides the detailed provisions).
>
> Aside from its legislative functions, some members of the House of Lords are senior judges and so, quite separately:
>
> - acts as the Supreme Court of Appeal (although, with legislation pending, this will end with the establishment of a separate supreme court).

died and were replaced by their succeeding heirs, as life peers died, or as successive prime ministers appointed new life peers, usually on political grounds. Its overall partisanship did not mirror that in the Commons. There are peers who support the Labour, Liberal Democrat and Conservative Parties, as well as a number of 'cross-benchers' who do not explicitly support any of these three parties. See Table 5.1 (overleaf), which also reveals the differences between the political affiliation of hereditary and life peers, as well as the overall composition of the House of Lords.

There are two main objections to the existing composition of the House of Lords. First, its unrepresentative composition and undemocratic basis. Second, the relatively permanent numerical advantage that was possessed by one party, the Conservatives, until 1999. Before then, hereditary peers, the large majority of them conservative by political inclination (small 'c') and Conservative by political affiliation (large 'C'), meant that the Labour Party could never have a Lords majority. Governments are based in the Commons and do not necessarily command majority support in the Lords. Legislation has to be passed in an agreed form by both the Commons and the Lords. The Lords may disagree with the Commons and amend legislation, whereupon the Commons has to decide whether to accept Lords amendments or to overturn them. How do you, or how should you, resolve differences between the two houses? This is a general problem in all bicameral political systems; it is not

TABLE 5.1   The composition of the House of Lords in late 2003 [1]

Party	Hereditary peers	Life peers	Total
Conservative	50	160	210
Labour	3	182	185
Liberal Democrat	5	59	64
Cross-bench	33	146	179
Others	–	7	7
Total	91	554	645

[1] The table does not include:

(i)   13 peers who were on leave of absence; 1 vacant hereditary peerage seat

(ii)   2 archbishops and 24 bishops of the Church of England who sit as members of the House of Lords; they bring the membership of the house to 671

(iii) others: 3 non-affiliated, 1 Green Party, 1 Independent Conservative, 1 Independent Labour, and 1 Independent Socialist.

one that is specific to the UK. However, in other such polities, for example as in the USA, where the House of Representatives and the Senate have to decide together the content of legislation (except for ratifying international treaties, which is the prerogative of the Senate alone), both legislative houses enjoy a democratic legitimacy. This the House of Lords at present plainly lacks.

One part of a solution to this problem was the Salisbury Convention, where the Lords agreed not to oppose a bill derived from a commitment in the election manifesto of the governing party. However, even here there could be elements of interpretation – how specific did the manifesto have to be? Labour governments, facing an upper house in which the Conservatives have a major presence, continue to have legislative problems. Should the issue be solved by adjusting the mechanism for resolving differences between the two chambers when they arise? Should the functions of the House of Lords be reformed? Or its composition? So, three fundamental questions lie behind reform of the Lords:

- Is a second chamber necessary?

- If there are two chambers, and the government derives its authority from its position in a popularly elected chamber, what should be the basis for the second chamber, and what should its powers be?

- Given particular powers and functions, what should be the relationship between the two legislative chambers? And how would conflicts between them be resolved?

We need to acknowledge that answers to these questions may draw on different kinds of evidence. With regard to the first question, there are democratic political systems that have only a one-chamber legislature, such as those of Denmark, Greece and New Zealand. Thus, having two chambers, retaining a House of Lords, is not necessarily essential. However, given the nature and extent of government in the UK, the system may function more effectively with two chambers that share the legislative load. Similar problems arise with the other questions too. There is also a further question: if you can reach agreement on reform, how do you move from the present House of Lords to a reformed one?

SUMMARY

- The House of Lords has a significant role in the current legislative process.
- Unlike the House of Commons, the House of Lords is unrepresentative and lacks a democratic mandate.
- Should a revised second chamber have a different composition – or different powers and responsibilities?

5 A BRIEF HISTORY OF LORDS REFORM

Governing and legislating in the UK involves the agreement of three institutions – the monarchy and the two Houses of Parliament. Over time the relative power of these three institutions has changed. With the development of mass democracy, expressed through popular elections to the House of Commons, the independent authority of the Crown has declined and many of its powers and prerogatives have passed to the executive, and to the prime minister as leader of the government. As illustrated in Chapter 1 the monarch now automatically grants assent to a bill that parliament presents. Of course, while the Commons derives its legitimacy and authority from a popular mandate, the Lords does not. Traditionally, it was composed of several elements: the lords spiritual (archbishops and bishops of the established Anglican church), together with the lords temporal (members of the hereditary peerage and a number of appointed life peers). The latter included senior judges who formed the Supreme Court of Appeal. Some of the problems with the House of Lords follow from its composition and from its ability to block decisions taken by the Commons – because of its composition its actions do at times seem to reflect a link to the traditional hierarchy of social privilege.

The political consequences of these differences became particularly noticeable with the growth of government legislation and the growing popular authority of the House of Commons. In 1909 the House of Lords rejected the budget put forward by the Liberal government. As a result, the 'non-democratic' second chamber was perceived as frustrating the will of the popularly based government. (Of course, at this time the franchise to elect the House of Commons was restricted to certain men and denied to all women.)

To resolve this problem King Edward VII indicated that if the government could win endorsement in a new election, he might be prepared to create enough new peers to give the government a majority in the Lords which then would enable the Liberals to pass reform legislation. After two elections in 1910 the re-elected Liberal government brought in the Parliament Act of 1911 to restrict the power of the Lords. The Act removed the power of the Lords to reject money bills, such as the budget, and reduced to two years its ability to delay other legislation that had been passed by the Commons. The bill was widely seen as a temporary measure, and in the preamble to the Act, the Liberal government expressed its intention to bring forward further legislation to reform both the composition of the Lords and the relationship between the Lords and Commons.

At the time, however, the parties could not reach agreement on the next stage of reform so the question lapsed. Thus, while the Parliament Act of 1911 preserved the House of Lords and enabled the legislative process to function, it left unanswered the three questions posed at the end of previous section. Since 1911 there have been some further adjustments, both to the composition and to the powers of the Lords. In 1949, a Labour government reduced its delaying powers over legislation to one year. A change in its composition followed from the passing of the Life Peers Act of 1958, which allowed for the appointment of non-hereditary members of the House of Lords. Such members are appointed by the prime minister, thus giving the prime minister wider powers of patronage. Finally, the Peerage Act of 1963 allowed peers to give up their titles, and their seats in the Lords, and seek election to the House of Commons.

Between 1949 and 1997 there was one major attempt to reform the Lords by a Labour government – the Parliament (No.2) Bill of 1968. Among other proposals it suggested that the reformed house should be appointed, not elected, with the government of the day having a small majority. The House would be divided into voting and non-voting members with about 230 voting members. It would evolve from the current House and could exercise a six-month delaying power on the passage of non-financial legislation. The measure failed to gain support from the backbenchers on both sides of the house. They objected to the extension of patronage in an appointed house and to the proposed increased power for the cross-benchers in the reformed chamber. The measure was opposed by many Labour and Conservative backbenchers, became bogged down in Committee in the House of Commons, and was eventually abandoned. The failure of the 1968 reform has been attributed to 'an unwillingness by the elected House to permit reform of the unelected House, which, by rendering the Lords more publicly acceptable, might give it greater political authority' (Griffith and Ryle, 1989, p.456)

After this failed attempt at reform there was little agreement between the parties in the period up to 1997. Indeed, both used very different arguments to support particular reform policies. In the 1970s the Labour Party was committed to the abolition of the House of Lords. This was prompted by the Lords repeated amendment of legislation introduced by successive Labour governments. It was argued that the actions of the Lords were politically biased and that it was more likely to amend or reject legislation from a Labour government than from a Conservative one. This in turn was seen as a direct result of its socially privileged composition, the fact that the interests of its members were necessarily different from those of the wider society. These differences were not just social. Women and those from minority ethnic backgrounds were also under-represented. Additionally, while there were 26 senior clerics from the Church of England in the House of Lords, other faiths had no such automatic representation. Conservative governments, and the Conservative Party generally, had fewer problems with the existing House of Lords, and so reform of the second chamber was never a central element of the party's policy agenda. Since the second chamber was a useful element of the legislative process, they argued that it should be retained. While they would probably agree that you would not now create a second chamber in its present form, Conservatives stressed the continuing need for a second chamber, the utility of the current arrangements, and the 'legitimacy' of a chamber that is the result of a long evolution.

The UK is essentially a unitary state. However, the establishment of some elements of devolved government in Scotland, Wales and Northern Ireland may decrease the centralization of political power and decision making, a process that could be taken further with the creation of a regional level of government in England (see Chapter 2). Indeed, the Liberal Democrats argue that the process should be extended and that a revised second chamber should represent the nations and regions of the UK and that it should be based on territorial representation as happens in federal political systems such as Australia and the USA. They suggest that in reforming the House of Lords one could draw on other examples of institutional design.

The expectation was that the Labour government, backed by a strong popular mandate in 1997, would be radical over constitutional reform. Indeed, as demonstrated above, there has been change in several areas. But for the House of Lords, unlike for devolution, the government did not have a clear set of institutional objectives. It was

'Aren't you going about constitutional reform in a rather reckless way, Mr Fawkes?'

One attempt at reform of the Lords?

committed only to creating a 'more democratic and representative' chamber, by removing the hereditary peers in the first instance. Its reform programme has proceeded in stages; indeed, ministers have sought to forge such a programme as they went along. Once the majority of the hereditary peers were removed, the government, faced with clear cross-party and intra-party disagreement over reform, tried to create a consensus through a Royal Commission charged with considering the role, function and composition of the reformed House of Lords (Figure 5.4). The Commission was made up of representatives of the three main parties together with independent members, was chaired by a former Conservative Cabinet minister, Lord Wakeham, and it consulted widely.

"Furthermore, we've enough port and brandy for six months!"

FIGURE 5.4 Lords' resistance to constitutional change

The Wakeham Commission proposed that the reformed House of Lords should be a revising chamber with a role that is complementary to that of the House of Commons (Royal Commission on the Reform of the House of Lords, 2000). The supremacy of the Commons would therefore be maintained. These suggestions were broadly accepted by all parties. In addition, the Commission recommended that the reformed chamber have an elected element, representing the nations and regions of the UK, comprising between 12 per cent and 35 per cent of the membership. After the 2001 election, when the government had promised to further pursue Lords reform, the Lord Chancellor's Department produced a White Paper, *Completing the Reform*, proposing that 20 per cent of the membership should be elected. This was widely seen as a retreat from Labour's initial commitment to reform, primarily in an attempt to gain broader political support. Among other critics, the Commons Public Administration Select Committee suggested that the proposals had too small a proportion of elected members. In response, Lord Irvine, the Lord Chancellor, then declared that a hybrid house – part elected and part appointed – would be unworkable. Subsequently, once it was clear that a large number in the Parliamentary Labour Party would not support the 20 per cent elected proposal, the government set up a Joint Parliamentary Committee of both Commons and Lords to further explore the issue and present wider proposals. In the event, the Committee recommended the Commons choose one of seven possible options. These ranged from 100% elected to 100% appointed chamber, with varying options in between: 80% appointed/20% elected; 60% appointed/40% elected; 80% elected/20% appointed; 60% elected/40% appointed; and 50% elected/50% appointed (Gamble, 2003). Before the Commons debate, the Prime Minister threw his support behind a wholly appointed chamber, but all of these alternatives were rejected by the House of Commons in February 2003, although a proposal for a chamber with 80% of elected members failed by only 3 votes (McLean *et al.*, 2003). This stalemate, on a free Commons vote, demonstrated the difficulty of reaching an agreement that was acceptable to all sides.

Most commentators assumed that the absence of any such consensus demonstrated that root-and-branch House of Lords reform was now a dead issue for the foreseeable future, and certainly for the remainder of the 2001 parliament. In October 2003, however, the government made plain its intention to legislate to remove the 92 remaining hereditary members and to transfer the power of the prime minister to appoint peers to a statutorily based independent appointment commission. The prime minister would retain the right to nominate the holders of certain offices as members of the revised chamber, and the Appointments Commission would propose new members subject to a requirement that 'the House of Lords should better reflect the make up of UK society ... guided in its decisions on the appropriate balance of new nominations between the parties, by the distribution of the vote between the major parties at the previous general election' (Department of Constitutional Affairs, 2003). This reflects ideas of democratic representation, but only in an indirect manner. The two major opposition parties, the Conservatives and the Liberal Democrats, continue to support the idea of a large elected element in the reformed chamber, as do many Labour MPs. In the short term, then, apart from the government's intention to remove the remaining hereditary peers (perhaps converting the most politically active hereditary peers into life peers), there is no agreement on the future role, function and composition of the second chamber. As a result, the reform of the House of Lords remains incomplete seven years into a Labour government and almost a century after the passage of the Parliament Act of 1911.

SUMMARY

- The reform of the House of Lords has been a lengthy, protracted and contested process.
- Previous attempts at reform have failed through disagreements both within and among the major parties.
- After 1997 the Labour government embarked on an extensive programme of constitutional reform.
- To achieve reform of the Lords the government has sought agreement with the other parties.

6 CONCLUSION

Although the reform of the House of Lords is still unfinished, what does this case study of constitutional change tell us about the nature of arguments in British politics and the use of evidence? In Chapter 1 (Section 5), Richard Heffernan stressed the flexibility of the constitution and suggested that 'reform, whatever other motivations might lay behind it, is ultimately facilitated by majoritarian politics'. He implied that a government with a parliamentary majority should be able to enact its legislative programme, and that includes constitutional reform. Indeed, this has been the case for all the reforms listed above in Box 5.2, including devolution, the incorporation of the ECHR into UK law and the reform of some aspects of the electoral process. But all of these changes were either known in some detail before the 1997 election or were the result of agreed external commitments. This is not true for the reform of the House of Lords.

Although the commitment to reform was known, there was no agreement either within the Labour Party or between the government and the opposition, about the details for reform. So while the government has a large majority, and can argue that it has a mandate for reform, it has been relatively unwilling to use its party majority in these circumstances. Instead, it has sought agreement with the main opposition parties and with its own backbench MPs. Although the government did act unilaterally to end the right of most hereditary peers to sit in the Lords in 1999 (with the support of all Labour MPs) a consensus has been sought through the appointment of a Royal Commission and in the use of a Joint Parliamentary Committee to introduce proposals after that Commission had reported.

Why should this be so? Part of an answer derives from the flexibility and uncodified nature of the UK constitution. Under a codified constitution, such as that of the USA, there is a prescribed process for constitutional change. This is not the case in the UK. For contested constitutional change, such as that of

Lords reform, the process only finishes when there is broad agreement among the parties on the ends of reform and on the nature of the revised second chamber. The lack of any agreement has meant that the Labour government's actions in this area have been in marked contrast to its use of its majority position to create new institutions in other areas of constitutional reform. If the government continues to seek broad agreement with the other parties then the current reform initiative may well end like that of 1911 with only a partially reformed house and no agreement on the final composition or powers of a second chamber.

What other conclusions can we draw from the arguments over Lords reform?

- First, that in discussing reform the different parties have used different types of argument and supported those arguments with different types of evidence.

- Second, that there is partial agreement on two of the three questions posed at the end of section 4. To recap, these were the three questions:

- Do we need a second chamber?

- If there are two chambers, and the government derives its authority from its position in a popularly elected chamber, what should be the basis for the second chamber, and what should its powers be?

- Given particular powers and functions, what should be the relationship between the two legislative chambers, and how would conflicts between them be resolved?

All the parties agree on the need for bicameralism, for retaining a second chamber. There is agreement too on the continuing supremacy of the House of Commons. The major differences both within and among the parties are over the composition of a reformed second chamber. Four options have been put forward:

- maintaining the status quo

- creating an appointed house

- creating an elected house

- creating a house that combines some element of appointment and election.

As the supremacy of the Commons is to be retained, this probably means that agreement on a wholly elected house is unlikely because the reformed Lords might then have the electoral legitimacy to challenge the Commons. However, a partly elected House of Lords could be both more legitimate and more representative than the present House, as it would reflect citizen preferences expressed through the ballot box. Of course, a wholly or largely appointed Lords, lacking legitimacy, would be a far weaker institution than one which had a large elected element.

One characteristic of reforms since 1997 has been the use of different electoral systems for different political institutions. As Mads Qvortrup notes in Chapter 3, the UK uses the single member plurality system (SMPS) in House of Commons elections, the additional member system (AMS) for elections to the devolved institutions for Scotland and Wales, a form of list proportional representation (PR) for elections to the European Parliament, and the single transferable vote (STV) for the Northern Ireland Assembly. So the principle of using different electoral systems for different institutions, with outcomes different from those that might be produced by the traditional and established SMPS, is now well established (Chapter 3; see also Curtice, 2003). Although it runs the risk of making a reformed House of Lords more representative than an unreformed House of Commons, the use of PR could also help to ensure that no single party would have an overall majority among the elected members. Such objectives have been set out by the government in one of its latest consultation documents (Department of Constitutional Affairs, 2003).

In addition, there may be an emerging partial consensus on the basis of elections for the reformed chamber. Both the Conservatives and the Liberal Democrats favour a mode of election that is regionally based, but they disagree on the electoral system that should be used. This disagreement is strictly on grounds of party interest. The Liberal Democrats favour PR, as this would maximize their representation, while the Conservatives prefer SMPS, which gives some advantages to the two larger parties and would reduce third party representation.

Are there any other areas of agreement among the parties? The revised second chamber plays no role in determining the choice of government. It does not, therefore, need to be elected at the same time or on the same basis as the Commons. It could be elected for a fixed term to make it more independent of government; all other elections – for local councils, devolved parliaments or assemblies and the European Parliament – are for fixed terms. Taken together, these features may suggest a possible future composition for a revised second chamber, but for any further change there does need to be broad agreement among the parties. As the constitution is, in theory, easily changed then such agreement will be needed to produce an agreed and stable outcome. We can see, therefore, that the reform of the House of Lords will only be complete when a new consensus on its powers and composition is reached, a consensus to which both evidence and argument contribute.

REFERENCES

Curtice, J. (2003) 'Changing voting systems' in Dunleavy, P., Gamble, A., Heffernan, R. and Peele, G. (eds).

Department of Constitutional Affairs (2003) *Constitutional Reform: Next Steps for the House of Lords*, CP14/03, London, Department of Constitutional Affairs.

Dunleavy, P., Gamble, A., Heffernan, R. and Peele, G. (eds) (2003) *Developments in British Politics 7*, London, Palgrave Macmillan.

Finer, S.E. (ed.) (1979) *Five Constitutions: Contrast and Comparisons*, Harmondsworth, Penguin.

Gamble, A. (2003) 'Remaking the constitution' in Dunleavy, P., Gamble, A., Heffernan, R. and Peele, G. (eds) (2003) *Developments in British Politics 7*, London, Palgrave Macmillan.

Griffith, J.A.G. and Ryle, M. (1989) *Parliament: Functions, Practices and Proceedings,* London, Sweet and Maxwell.

Hirschman, A.O. (1970) *Exit, Voice and Loyalty: Responses to Decline in Firms, Organizations, and States*, Cambridge, Mass., Harvard University Press.

May, T.E. (1997; first published 1844) *Erskine May's Treatise on the Law, Privileges, Proceedings and Usage of Parliament* (22nd edition), edited by Limon, Sir Donald and McKay, W.R, London, Butterworths.

McLean, I., Spirling, A. and Russell, M. (2003) 'None of the above: the UK House of Commons votes on reforming the House of Lords', *Political Quarterly*, vol.74, no.3, pp.298–310.

Powell, E. (1978) Seminar on devolution, Nuffield College, Oxford.

Tsebelsis, G. and Money, J. (1997) *Bicameralism,* New York, Cambridge University Press.

Royal Commission on the Reform of the House of Lords (2000) *A House for the Future*, Cm 4534, London, The Stationery Office (Wakeham Report).

FURTHER READING

Finer, S.E. (ed.) (1979) *Five Constitutions: Contrast and Comparison*, Harmondsworth, Penguin, outlines the constitutions of Britain, France and the USA (amongst others); it is updated in Finer, S.E., Bogdanor, V. and Rudden, B. (eds) (1995) *Comparing Constitutions*, Oxford, Oxford University Press. For a survey of the modern British constitution see Bogdanor, V. (ed.) (2003) *The British Constitution in the Twentieth Century*, Oxford, Oxford University Press; the chapter by R. Walters covers the House of Lords. He discusses attempts at reform on pages 228–35 and suggests that three factors have contributed to its failure: a lack of political commitment to reform, disagreements between the major parties, and disagreements between the two houses of parliament.

A more accessible account of reform after the election of the Labour government in 1997 is in the chapter by A. Gamble, 'Reforming the constitution' (pages 18–38) in Dunleavy, P., Gamble, A., Heffernan, R. and Peele, G. (eds) (2003) *Developments in British Politics 7*, London, Palgrave Macmillan.

The Wakeham Report, *A House for the Future* (The Report of the Royal Commission on the Reform of the House of Lords, 2000) is a key document in the recent reform of the second chamber. The evidence given by the three major parties to the commission outlines their position at the time and is on the CD that comes with the printed report.

An interestingly different analysis can be found in Wright, A. (2003) *British Politics. A Very Short Introduction*, Oxford, Oxford University Press. Wright is a politician with a commitment to constitutional reform and Chapter 2, 'The constitution', and Chapter 3, 'Arguing: the political conversation', are both relevant.

Acknowledgements

Grateful acknowledgement is made to the following sources for permission to reproduce material in this book.

Chapter 1

Figures

Figure 1.1: © IJO/Rex Features; Figure 1.2: © Hulton Archive; Figure 1.3: © James D. Morgan/Rex Features; Figure 1.4: © Bandphoto/UPPA; Figure 1.5: © Rex Features.

Chapter 2

Figures

Figure 2.1: © National Galleries of Scotland; Figure 2.2: By permission of Llyfrgell Genedlaethol Cymru/The National Library of Wales; Figure 2.3: © Nezumi Dumousseau; Figure 2.4: © Sutton-Hibbert/Rex Features.

Tables

Tables 2.1–2.4: The Electoral Commission.

Chapter 3

Figures

Figure 3.1: © PA Photos; Figure 3.2: © Peter MacDiarmid/Rex Features; Figure 3.3: © Steve Bell 2004.

Chapter 4

Tables

Table 4.1: *Social Capital: A Discussion Paper* (2002) Prime Minister's Strategy Unit. Crown copyright material is reproduced under Class Licence Number C01W0000065 with the permission of the Controller of HMSO and the Queen's Printer for Scotland; Table 4.2: *Eurobarometer*, No.57, Fieldwork: 1 March–1 May 2002, Full Report, p.7. European Communities.

Figures

Figure 4.1: © Rex Features; Figure 4.2: © Mike Partridge/Rex Features; Figure 4.3: © Tony Husband/Punch Cartoon Library; Figure 4.4: © EU Audiovisual Library; Figure 4.5: © Richard Jolley/Cartoon Stock.

Chapter 5

Figures

Figure 5.1: © Hulton Archive; Figure 5.2: © PA Photos; Figure 5.3 (left): © Bandphoto/UPPA; (right) © Dave Williams/Photolibrary Wales; Figure 5.4: © Raymond Jackson/*Evening Standard*. Courtesy of Centre for Study of Cartoons and Caricature, University of Kent.

Cartoon

p.159: © Matthew Pritchett/*Daily Telegraph*, courtesy of Centre for the Study of Cartoons and Caricature, University of Kent.

Cover

Image copyright © PhotoDisc, Inc.

Every effort has been made to contact copyright owners. If any have been inadvertently overlooked, the publishers will be pleased to make the necessary arrangements at the first opportunity.

Index

absolutist monarchy, and the
  transformation to parliamentary
  democracy 7, 8, 9
actors *see* political actors
age, and political participation 80
agenda-setting
    and the media 97, 101
    and policy networks 114
agriculture, policy-making in 114
Ahern, Bertie 60
Aldridge, S. 126
Alford Index of Class-Voting 92
Alfred, king of the English 44
Algeria, and constitutional reform in
  France 139–40
Almond, Gabriel 78
AMS (additional member system)
  33–4, 37, 89, 164
anti-globalization protests 77
Arbroath, Declaration of 45
associational democracy 119
associationism 112, 116, 118–19
asymmetric decentralization model
  56, 64
    and the Scottish Parliament 58
asymmetrically bicameral
  parliaments, and the UK 22, 36, 142
Athenian democracy 99–100
Attlee government, and class
  interests 109
Australia 12, 17, 145, 159
authoritarian states 9
authoritative works, and the UK
  constitution 19, 150
authority, and the constitutional
  order 11

Bagehot, Walter, *The English
  Constitution* 19, 22, 24
Bannockburn, Battle of (1314) 45
bargaining, and multi-level
  governance 124–5
Belfast, and centre–periphery
  relations 53, 54
Belfast (Good Friday) Agreement
  60–1, 64, 79, 82
bicameralism
    and the UK 22, 36, 142, 154,
    155–6, 163
    and the USA 36, 156

Blair, Tony 23, 27, 29
    and Northern Ireland 60
    and *The Sun* newspaper 95
BMA (British Medical Association)
  113
bonding social capital 126, 129
Bosworth Field, Battle of (1485) 46
Boyne, Battle of the (1690) 47, 48
bridging social capital 126, 129
Brighton bombing (1984) 82
Britain, history of 68–9
British Empire 69, 70
British Medical Association (BMA)
  113
British Social Attitudes Survey (BSAS)
  127
British–Irish Council 61
Britishness, concept of 70
Brooke, Peter 82
Bryson, Bill 78

Cabinet, and the prime minister 27
Callaghan, James 32
campaign activities, and political
  participation 77, 80, 81
Campaign for the English Regions 66
Campbell, Alastair 97
Camus, Albert, *L'Homme Revolté* 78
Canada, as a federal state 42
Catholicism
    and the British nation 68, 69
    in Ireland 47–9
    in Wales 47
centralized unitary states 42, 43
centre–periphery relations 3, 42–73
    and the making of the UK 44–9
    national identities and UK politics
    53–6
    in the USA 36
    see also devolution
Channel Islands 61
Charles I, King 9, 45
Charles II, King 45
Charlesworth, J. 113
Church of England
    senior clerics in the House of
    Lords 22, 142, 159
    and Wales 46
    see also religion
Churchill, Winston 32

citizens, and the state 1
citizenship, and the English language
  54
civil servants, and the government 26
civil society
    and policy networks 112
    and the state 1–2, 9
civil war (1640s) 9, 45
class
    class politics and public opinion
    97–8
    and elites 116
    and political participation 77, 85
    and voting patterns 91–5, 101
        and economic voting 94
        'revisionist' alternative 93
        traditional model of 91–2
class interests 109
Clinton, Bill 29, 60
club rules, and constitutional reform
  138–9, 141
coalition governments, and SMPS
  (single member plurality system)
  32, 33
Cole, G.D.H. 118
collective interests 108–9
collegial executives 28, 30
Colley, Linda, on the British nation
  68–9
'commitology', and European Union
  decision making 121–3
common law, and the UK
  constitution 19, 149
Commonwealth countries, and the
  English language 54
communal activities, and political
  participation 77, 81
comparative politics 4
conflict among interests 109–10
consensus democracies 13, 14–16,
  34, 38
    electoral systems 14, 31
    and the UK 37
    and the USA 16, 35, 36
Conservative Party
    and the 2001 general election 32
    and class voting patterns 92, 93,
    101
    and constitutional reform 145,
    146, 147–8, 150

House of Lords 156, 159, 161, 164
and devolution 147–8, 149
and economic voting 94
and the news media 96
and party identifiers 86, 87, 88
and public opinion 98
and referendums 84
and SMPS (single member plurality system) 32, 33
and the UK party system 34
constitutional monarchy in the UK 7, 8
constitutional reform 4, 20, 138–64
and club rules 138–9, 141
and devolution 147–8, 150, 159, 162
and executive–legislative relations 21
in France 139–40
major initiatives since 1997 150–2
and political argument 141–6
'pragmatic' arguments 143–5, 146, 152
'system design' arguments 144–5
'underlying principles' arguments 143, 146, 152
and the political parties 145–6, 147–8, 152–3
and the UK political system 140–1
in the United States 140
constitutions
EU constitution 72
flexible and inflexible 11, 14, 16
and liberal democracies 11, 17–21
in majoritarian and consensus democracies 14
and networks 108
structures imposed by 6
UK constitution 3, 18, 19–20, 21, 22
five sources of the 19
as flexible 18, 19, 35, 36, 37, 38, 140, 162
principles and conventions 148–53
US constitution 16, 18–19, 21
Cornish language 70
corporate interests 1, 2, 10
corporatism, and policy networks 112, 116, 117–18
Countryside Alliance 77, 79
Cromwell, Oliver 45, 46

cultural homogenization, and nation-states 51, 52
Curtice, John 93
custom and practice, and the UK constitution 19

Dalyell, Tam 64
de-alignment, and party identifiers 87
decentralized unitary states 42–3
symmetric and asymmetric 56
Delors Committee 122, 123, 124
democracy
associative 118, 119
Athenian 99–100
and the constitutional order 11
and constitutional reform, arguments based on 'democratic principles' 143, 146, 152
and elite networks 116
and House of Lords reform 154
and the nation-state 51
and political networks 129–30
and political participation 76
and social capital 126–7
see also representative democracy
Denmark 157
designer politics 98–100, 102
deviating elections, and non-party identifiers 86
devolution 15, 33, 37, 38, 43
and centre–periphery relations 42–3, 56–64
and constitutional reform 147–8, 150, 159, 162
critics of 64
and the English regions 65–7
and the European Union 71–3
functions reserved for UK Parliament and government 63
funding 63
London 65
in Northern Ireland 56, 60–2, 66
and policy networks 133
referendums on 57, 58, 59, 61, 65
in Scotland 15, 20, 55, 56, 57–9, 66
and shared identity 67
in Wales 15, 20, 55, 56, 60–2, 66
and the 'West Lothian question' 64
see also National Assembly for Wales; Northern Ireland Assembly; Scottish Parliament
Dicey, A.V., Introduction to the Study of the Law of the Constitution 19
Disraeli, Benjamin 25

dissent
illegal mass protest 77, 78
and NGOs (non-governmental organizations) 113, 116, 119–20
and political participation 77, 78–9, 102
and terrorism in the UK 81–2
Douglas-Home, Alec 27
Downs, Anthony 89

Eastern Europe 77
ECHR see European Convention of Human Rights (ECHR)
economic voting 94
Edinburgh, and centre–periphery relations 53, 54
education
and nation-states 52
policy-making in 114
educational background, and political participation 77, 80–1, 84, 85, 101
Edward I, King of England 45, 46
Edward II, King of England 45
Edward VII, King 158
Eisenhower, Dwight 86
Elazar, D. 42
Electoral Commission 151, 152
electoral franchise
and the House of Commons 20, 22
and voting rights in the UK 16–17
and women 17
electoral systems 11, 163–4
AMS (additional member system) 33–4, 37, 89, 164
in majoritarian and consensus democracies 14
proportional representation (PR) 32, 33–4, 89, 164
single member plurality system (SMPS) 3, 15, 31–4, 37, 163–4
single transferable vote (STV) 164
and voter turnout 89
electoral turnout
country comparisons of 89, 90
declining rates of 85, 88, 101
and party identifiers 87
see also voting behaviour
elite networks 112, 116–17, 129, 138
Elizabeth I, Queen of England 46
Elizabeth II, Queen 8 59
Engels, F. 91
England
and centre–periphery relations 53–4

English identity 70
regional government in 65–7
and the UK 6, 7, 44
English language, and centre–periphery relations 53, 54
Enlightenment, and constitutions 18
epistemic networks 123
ethnicity, and nation-states 51–2
Eurobarometer Survey, on political participation 78
European Commission 128
European Convention of Human Rights (ECHR) 149, 151, 152, 162
European Council, and the Delors Committee 122, 123, 124
European Parliament 151, 164
European Union (EU) 3, 10
and Britishness 70
Committee of the Regions 72
decision making and 'commitology' 121–3
and the delegation of power by parliament 20
and devolution 71–3
European law
and the House of Commons 23
and the UK constitution 19, 20, 149
and the 'Four Motors of Europe' 71–2
Structural Funds 71
and trust in political institutions, attitudes of different countries 127–8
and UK constitutional reform 151, 152
UK membership 7, 15, 38
and centre–periphery relations 43, 72–3
executive government
functions 11
in majoritarian and consensus democracies 14, 34
in the UK (Whitehall) 15, 21, 25, 26–30, 34, 35, 36, 37
in the USA 16–17, 35, 36
executive–legislative relations
and the constitution 18
in majoritarian and consensus democracies 14
in the UK 21–6, 28, 29, 36, 37
in the USA 36

Falkirk, Battle of (1298) 45
federal states 12, 13, 42

and consensus democracies 14
and executive–legislative relations 21
power and sovereignty in 43
and the US system of government 15–16
'feel-good factor', and voting behaviour 94
Figgis, J.N. 118
First World War 49, 69
Flanders 55, 71, 72
flexibility of the UK constitution 18, 19, 35, 36, 37, 38, 140, 162
flexible constitutions, and the UK 18, 19, 35
focus groups 97, 98, 100, 102
France
constitution 18
the Algerian crisis and constitutional reform 139–40
political participation and protest in 78, 81
political system 12
as a unitary state 42
women and voting rights 17
fuel tax protesters (2000) 79, 97, 114, 115
Fukuyama, Frances 126

Gaelic language 70
gender, and political participation 81
Germany
Bundesrat (upper house) 144
constitutions 18
electoral turnout 89
as a federal state 42
political participation in 78
political system 12
symmetric decentralization in 56
Gieben, B. 11
Giscard d'Estaing, Valery 72
globalization
and corporatism 118
and nation-states 51, 52
and national government 2
Glyndwr, Owain 46
Goldsmith, Sir James 84
Goldthorpe, John 92–3
Gould, Philip 97
governance
and networks 108
private-interest 132
see also multi-level governance
government
'joined-up' 116

limits to 38
and policy choices 2
and the state 1
Greece 157
Greenpeace 79
group interest 109

Hague, William 98
Heath, Anthony 93
Henry VII, King of England 46
Henry VIII, King of England 8, 46
hereditary peers
in the House of Lords 22, 154, 156, 162
and constitutional reform 142–3, 145, 146, 151, 160, 161
hierarchical organizations, and policy networks 130, 131, 132
Hirschman, A.O. 138–9
Hirst, Paul 118
historical political tradition in the UK 6–10
Hooghe, L. 123
horizontal policy coordination, and multi-level governance 121
House of Commons
and the constitution 144
and constitutional conventions 149
and executive–legislative relations 21, 22, 23, 24–5
and the extension of the electoral franchise 20, 22
and the House of Lords 154, 155, 157, 163
membership and functions 23
and the prime minister 27, 30
and SMPS (single member plurality system) 34, 37
House of Lords 21
and constitutional conventions 149
and constitutional reform 22, 153, 154–64
history of 157–61
Parliament (No.2) Bill (1968) 158–9
and political argument 141–6
problems of 156–7
Wakeham Commission on 160
contemporary functions of 154, 155
membership and functions 22
political party representation in 155, 156

and the prime minister 27
Humphreys, W.D. 113

identity
    and Britishness 70
    devolution and shared identity 67
India 42
individual executives 28, 30
individual interests 108, 109
Industrial Revolution, and Wales 47
informal rationality, and networks 130
Inglehart, Ronald 92
interest groups, and the state 1, 2, 10
international corporations 1
international political actors 10
Internet voting 82
IRA (Irish Republican Army) 49, 60, 62, 82
    bombing campaign in Britain 79
Ireland
    and the British Empire 69
    Easter Rising (1916) 49
    Great Famine (1840s) 48
    Home Rule 49
    partition of 49
    and the UK 6, 7, 47–9
    as a unitary political system 12
    War of Independence (1919–21) 49
Irvine, Lord 161
Isle of Man 61
issue networks 113, 114, 124
issue voting 93
    and economic voting 94
Italy
    social capital in 126–7, 128
    as a unitary state 42

James II, King of England 47
James VI, King of Scotland (and I of England) 45, 46, 49
Japan 18
John Balliol, King of Scotland 45
John XXII, Pope 45
Johnson, President Lyndon 28
'joined-up' government 116
Jowell, Roger 93
judicial reviews
    in majoritarian and consensus democracies 14, 37
    in the United States 16, 20
judiciary
    Court of Great Session in Wales 46
    functions 11
    in the UK 15, 36

Supreme Court of Appeal 155, 157
    in the United States 16–17, 36

Key, V.O. 94

Labour Party
    and the 2001 general election 27, 32
    and class voting patterns 92, 93, 101
    and constitutional reform 142–3, 145, 146, 147–8, 150–2, 153
        House of Lords 155, 156, 159–61, 164
    and devolution 20, 33
    and economic voting 94
    and the European Union 83
    and the National Assembly for Wales 60
    and party identifiers 86–7, 88
    and the prime minister 27
    and referendums 84
    and the Scottish Constitutional Convention 57
    and the Scottish Parliament 33, 58, 60
    and SMPS (single member plurality system) 32, 33
    and The Sun newspaper 95–6
    and the UK party system 34
Laski, Harold 118
legislatures
    functions 11
    in majoritarian and consensus democracies 14
    policy-influencing 24
    policy-making 23
    proactive 24
    reactive 24
    in the UK 15, 36, 37
    in the USA 16–17, 36
    see also executive–legislative relations; parliament
legitimacy
    and the constitutional order 11
    and the nation 50
Lewis, P. 11, 78, 81, 85
liberal democracies
    different state structures in 6
    government in 10–13
    and the historical political tradition in the UK 6–10
    networks of political power and authority in 112–13

state–society relations in 1–2
    see also consensus democracies; majoritarian democracies
Liberal Democrats
    and the 2001 general election 32
    and constitutional reform 145, 153
        House of Lords 155, 156, 159, 161, 164
    and the devolved assemblies in Scotland and Wales 33
    and the National Assembly for Wales 60
    and the news media 96–7
    and the Scottish Constitutional Convention 57
    and the Scottish Parliament 33, 58, 60
    and SMPS (single member plurality system) 32, 33
    as a 'third party' 34
Liberal Party (UK) 32–3
life peers
    in the House of Lords 22, 155, 156
    and constitutional reform 142, 150
Lijphart model
    of majoritarian and consensus democracies 14
    and the UK 37
linking social capital 126, 129
lobbying 2
    and corporatism 117
local government
    and the state 9
    in the UK 15
Locke, John 18
London
    and centre–periphery relations 43, 53, 54
    Greater London Authority (GLA) 65, 151

Maastricht Treaty, and the Committee of the Regions 72
Macmillan, Harold 27, 38, 97
McQuail, P. 66
maintaining elections, and party identifiers 86
Major, John 28, 32
majoritarian democracies 13, 14–16
    advantages and disadvantages of 38
    electoral systems 14, 31, 32
    and the UK 14–15, 20, 34, 35–8

compared with the USA 35, 36
and the prime minister 28
and the two party system 33, 34
and the United States 16
managerialism, and policy networks 132–3
Mandelson, Peter 97
manufacturing employment, and social class 92
market economy, and the state 2, 9
market mechanisms, and policy networks 132–4
market power, and policy networks 130, 131
Marks, G. 123
Marquand, David 66
Marx, K. 91
May, Erskine
  Parliamentary Practice 19
  Treatise on the Law, Privileges, Proceedings and Usage of Parliament 150
media
  and nation-states 52
  see also news media
media organizations 1
Michigan School of party identification 85–7, 93, 94
miners' strike (1984/5) 79
Mitchell, Senator George 60
monarchy
  and Britishness 70
  in England 44
  erosion of political power 7–9, 20
  and the House of Lords 157
  and the prime minister 27
  and the UK parliament 21, 22
Money, J. 154
Montesquieu, C. de 18
Mowlam, Mo 60
MPs (members of parliament)
  and the constitution 20
  and executive–legislative relations 23, 25–6
  and the prime minister 27, 30
  and the 'West Lothian question' 64
multi-level governance 121–5
  and European Union decision making 121–3
  power sharing and jurisdictions 123–5
Murdoch, Rupert 95

nation
  concept of the 50–1
  nations without states, and the European Union 71, 72
nation-states 51–2
  and the European regional movement 73
  and political institutions 139
National Assembly for Wales 20, 43, 59, 151
  and the AMS (additional member system) 33, 37
  and constitutional reform 145, 150, 151
  election results 60
  functions 63
  referendum on (1997) 59
  and Westminster 34
national corporations 1
National Federation for the Self-Employed 79
National Government (1931–35) 32
National Health Service 133
national interest 109, 111
nationalist movements, in Scotland and Wales 55
negotiated interests, and elite networks 117
negotiation, and multi-level governance 124–5
neo-corporatism, and policy networks 132
networks 3–4, 106–35
  aspects of political networks 106–8
  associations 106
  elites 106
  and governance 108
  and political interests 108–11
  of political power and authority 112–13
  see also policy networks
New Zealand 157
news media 3, 9, 38
  and the 1997 general election 95–7
  and political participation 76, 101–2
  and spin doctors 98–9
NGOs (non-governmental organizations) 113, 116, 119–20, 131
Nixon, Richard 29

non-governmental organizations *see* NGOs
non-state organizations 1
Norman invasions of England 44
Northern Ireland
  Belfast (Good Friday) Agreement 60–1, 64, 79, 82
  British–Irish Council 61
  and Britishness 70
  and centre–periphery relations 54–5
  Democratic Unionist Party (DUP) 62
  devolution in 56, 60–2
  formation of 49
  North–South Ministerial Council 61
  Omagh bombing 62
  Plantation of Ulster 47
  political participation in 81–2, 84
  referendums on the peace process 61
  religious discrimination in 47–9
  and the UK 6, 7, 47–9
Northern Ireland Assembly 43, 61–2
  election results 62
  functions 63
  suspension of 62
  voting system 164

Oakeshott, Michael 84
O'Connell, Daniel 48
OECD (Organization of Economic Cooperation and Development) 125
'old boy' networks 106, 107, 116, 130
OMC (open methods of coordination) 121, 122
open methods of coordination (OMC) 121, 122
Orange Order 48
Organization of Economic Cooperation and Development (OECD) 125
overcrowded policy making 115

Paisley, Ian 62
parliament (Westminster)
  and the erosion of monarchical power 7–9, 20
  and executive–legislative relations 21–6
  non-separation of powers between government and 23, 25

and the prime minister 29
and the Scottish Parliament 34, 57
sovereignty of 19–20, 112
state opening of 8
and the UK constitution 19–20, 37, 38
see also House of Commons; House of Lords; MPs (members of parliament)
parliamentary state politics 3, 6–38
and the constitution 16–21
executive–legislative relations 21–6
and political systems 10–13
and the prime minister 26–30
and single member plurality system (SMPS) 3, 15, 31–4
parliamentary systems of government 12, 13
in the UK 15, 140
party identification, and voting behaviour 85–90
party systems 11
in majoritarian and consensus democracies 14
in the UK 37
nationalist parties 33, 34
and the single member plurality system (SMPS) 31–4
and two-party plus majoritarianism 33, 34
patronage, and the prime minister 25
Plato, *Protagonists* 99–100
pluralism, and political interests 109
policy areas, and the European Union 15
policy choices, and government 2
policy communities 113–14, 124
policy networks 3–4, 107, 112–35
and associationism 112, 116, 118–19
and concertation 112
and corporatism 112, 116, 117–18
and elites 112, 116–17, 129, 138
evaluation of 129–31
and the formation of public policy 113–20
and NGOs (non-governmental organizations) 113, 116, 119–20
and social capital 125–9, 134
state agencies and market mechanisms 132–4
see also multi-level governance; networks; policy networks
policy units 131, 133

policy-influencing legislatures 24
policy-making legislatures 23
political actors
and the constitution 11
and government 6, 10
in liberal democracies 35
state and non-state 10
political interests 108–11
conflict among 109–10
political opinion, and the state 2
political participation 76–102
assessing 80–5
and class 77, 85, 91–5, 101
and educational background 77, 80–1, 84, 85, 101
extra-parliamentary activities 79, 84, 102
forms of 77
and gender 81
motivations for 77–9
in Northern Ireland 81–2, 84
and party identification 85–90
and public opinion 97–100, 102
and referendums 83–4
surveys on 78, 100
and terrorism in the UK 81–2
political parties (UK) 1, 2, 9
and constitutional reform 145–6, 147–8, 152–3
and the Electoral Commission 151, 152
in the House of Lords 155, 156
and 'instrumentalist' voters 84
membership of 80, 98, 100, 102
party identification and voters 85–90
and the prime minister 27, 28
and public opinion 97–100
Referendum Party 84
see also Conservative Party; Labour Party; Liberal Democrats; party systems
politics, defining 1
polycentric multi-level governance 123–4
power
centralized power and absolute power 9–10
erosion of monarchical power 7–9
and issue networks 114
networks of political power and authority 112–13
of parliament 20
and policy making 116
of the prime minister 27–9, 35

constraints on 28–9
royal prerogative powers 149
in unitary and federal states 43
power sharing and jurisdictions, and multi-level governance 123–5
PR *see* proportional representation (PR)
'pragmatic' arguments, for constitutional reform 143–5, 146, 152
presidential systems of government 12, 13
and executive–legislative relations 21
and prime ministers 28
in the United States 12, 15–16, 35, 36
and the UK prime minister 28, 29, 30
pressure groups 1, 2
prime minister (UK) 26–30
compared with the US president 29, 30
and electoral performance 31
and executive–legislative relations 23, 25, 29
and government ministers 26, 27, 28, 29
and the House of Lords 143, 155, 161
and parliamentary democracy 8, 9
and power 27–9, 35
constraints on 28–9
and royal prerogative powers 149
private-interest governance 132
proactive legislatures 24
procedural rationality, and networks 130
Prokhovnik, R. 24
proportional representation (PR) 32, 164
AMS (additional member system) 33–4
and electoral turnout 89
Protestantism
and the British nation 68–9
in Northern Ireland 47–9
psephology, and party identifiers 87
public opinion
and government policy 2, 3
and the news media 97
organization of 97–100, 102
and political actors 6
public–private partnerships 133
Putnam, R.D. 126, 128

quangos (quasi-governmental organizations) 131, 133

racial discrimination, and voting rights 17
rational choice theory, and voting 89, 93
re-aligning elections, and party identification 86
reactive legislatures 24
Rebecca Riots (1843) 47
Rebel Without a Cause (film) 80
Referendum Party 84
referendums
    on constitutional reform in France 140
    on devolution 57, 58, 59, 61, 65
    on EU membership 83
    and political participation 83–4
Regional Chambers 66
Regional Development Agencies (RDAs) 65–6
religion
    and the British nation 68–9
    Catholicism 47–9, 68, 69
    Church of Scotland 45
    in Northern Ireland 47–9
    Protestantism 47–9, 68–9
    in Wales 46
religious discrimination, in Ireland 48–9
representative democracy
    and political interests 110–11
    and political networks 129
representative government 9
retrospective voting 94
Ridder, Rick 99
Robert the Bruce, King of Scotland 45
Romanticism, and national identity 69
Roosevelt, Franklin 86
Rousseau, Jean-Jacques 95, 97
royal prerogative powers, and the UK constitution 149
RSPB (Royal Society for the Protection of Birds) 80, 98

Salisbury Convention, and the UK constitution 149, 156
Salisbury, Lord 27
Sanders, David 94
Sandford, M. 66
Schmitter, P.C. 119

Scotland
    and the Act of Union (1707) 45, 49
    and centre–periphery relations 53, 54, 55, 58
    devolution in 15, 20, 55, 56, 57–9
        and the 1979 referendum 57
    distinctive culture and traditions 45, 58, 69
    localism in 69
    nationalism in 70
        and constitutional change 147–8
    and the UK 6, 7, 44–5
    union with England 7, 45, 69, 70
Scottish Constitutional Convention 57, 66
Scottish Nationalist Party (SNP) 55, 58, 147
Scottish Office 47
Scottish Parliament 151
    and the 1997 referendum 57, 58, 59
    and the AMS (additional member system) 33, 37
    and constitutional reform 145, 150, 151
    and devolution 20, 43, 57, 58
    election results (1999 and 2003) 58
    First Minister 57
    functions 57, 63
    and Regional Development Agencies 65
    tax-raising powers 59–60
    and Westminster 34, 57
sectorization, in policy making 115
semi-federalist multi-level governance 123
service sector employment, and social class 92
'signalling effect' of elections 84
single member plurality system (SMPS) 3, 15, 31–4, 37, 164
single transferable vote (STV) 164
Skelcher, C. 131
Smith, M.J. 31, 76, 77, 85, 89, 91
SMPS *see* single member plurality system (SMPS)
SNP (Scottish Nationalist Party) 55, 58, 147
social capital 125–9
    declining 101
    and European Union countries 127–8

and regional government in Italy 126–7
    transformation of 128–9
    types of 126
    and the UK government 126
social class *see* class
sophists, and Athenian democracy 99–100
Sorel, George, *Réflections sur la Violence* 78
sound bites 97
sovereignty
    and associationism 118
    and the constitutional order 11
    and the European Union 70
    of parliament 19–20, 112
    in unitary and federal states 43
Spain
    Catalonia 55, 67, 71, 72
    devolution in 43, 55, 67
    and the nation-state 51
    symmetric decentralization in 56
    as a unitary state 42
spin doctors 97, 98–9, 100
the state
    and civil society 1–2
    and the constitution 11
    and government 1, 6
    and the liberal tradition in the UK 9
    and the nation 50
    and policy making 115
statute law, and the UK constitution 19, 149
Stirling Bridge, Battle of (1297) 45
Streek, W. 119
STV (single transferable vote) 164
The Sun newspaper, and the 1997 general election 95–6
Switzerland 17, 42, 89
symmetric decentralization model 56
'system design' arguments, for constitutional reform 144–5

tactical voting, and SMPS (single member plurality system) 33
taxation
    revenue-raising powers 10
    and the Scottish Parliament 59
tele-voting 82
terrorism, and political participation or dissent 81–2
Thatcher governments, and individual interests 109

Thatcher, Margaret 28, 29, 82, 83
  and corporatism 118
think tanks 131
Tomaney, John 66
totalitarian states 9
trade unions
  and the Labour Party 97
  membership of, and political
    participation 80
Transport 2000 114
Truman, Harry 86
trust
  and policy networks 130
  and social capital 125, 126, 127–9
Tsebelis, G. 154

UK legislation
  Act of Union (1707) 45, 49
  Freedom of Information Act (1999)
    151
  Human Rights Act (1998) 151
  Life Peers Act (1958) 142, 158
  Parliament Act (1911) 142, 148,
    158, 161
  Parliament Act (1949) 150
  Peerage Act (1963) 158
'underlying principles' arguments, for
  constitutional reform 143, 146, 152
unitary states 12, 13
  and executive–legislative relations
    21
  and majoritarian democracies 14
  power and sovereignty in 43
  and the UK 35, 140
    transformation to decentralized
    unitary state 42–3
United Kingdom (UK)
  history of the making of 44–9
  structure of the 6–7

United Nations (UN) 10
United States of America
  Congress 20, 23
    and impeachment 29
  constitution 16, 18–19, 21
    provisions for amendment 140
  electoral turnout 89
  as a federal state 42
  House of Representatives 144, 156
  presidential elections, and party
    identification 86
  presidential system of government
    12, 15–16, 35, 36
    compared with the UK prime
    minister 28, 29, 30
  Senate 144, 156
  and social capital 128
  Supreme Court 16, 20, 36
  universal suffrage 17
  women and voting rights 17
universal suffrage 17

Valera, Eamon de 49
Verba, Sidney 78
vertical policy coordination, and
  multi-level governance 121
Viking invasions of England 44
voting behaviour
  and class 91–5, 101
  instrumentalist voters 84
  and the news media 95–7, 101–2
  paradox of 89
  and party identification 85–90
    UK general elections (1964–
    2001) 88
  and political participation 77, 82
  see also referendums
voting rights see electoral franchise
voting systems see electoral systems

Wakeham Commission, on House of
  Lords reform 160
Wales
  and the Act of Union (1536) 46
  and centre–periphery relations 55
  devolution in 15, 20, 55, 56, 60–2
  distinctiveness of 69
  and the European Union (EU) 72
  incorporation into England 44, 69,
    70
  nationalism in 46, 70
    and constitutional change 147–
    8
  and the UK 6, 7, 46–7
  see also National Assembly for
    Wales
Wallace, William 45
war
  and the British nation 68
  and the UK government 2
Welsh language 70
Welsh Office 47
Westminster see parliament
  (Westminster)
William I, King of England (the
  Conqueror) 44
William III, King of England 47–8
Wilson, Harold 117, 118, 147
Wilson, Woodrow 86
women
  in the House of Lords 159
  and political participation 81
  and voting rights 17
World Bank 125
World Values Survey (WVS) 78, 127

younger people, and political
  participation 80